1

College
Reading

College Reading

1

ENGLISH FOR ACADEMIC SUCCESS

Cheryl Benz
Georgia Perimeter College

WITH Myra M. Medina
Miami Dade College

SERIES EDITORS

Patricia Byrd

Joy M. Reid

Cynthia M. Schuemann

HEINLE
CENGAGE Learning™

Australia • Brazil • Japan • Korea • Mexico • Singapore • Spain • United Kingdom • United States

HEINLE
CENGAGE Learning

College Reading 1
English for Academic Success
Benz/Medina

Publisher: Patricia A. Coryell
Director of ESL Publishing: Susan Maguire
Senior Development Editor: Kathy Sands Boehmer
Editorial Assistant: Evangeline Bermas
Senior Project Editor: Kathryn Dinovo
Manufacturing Assistant: Karmen Chong
Senior Marketing Manager: Annamarie Rice
Design/Production: LaurelTech
Cover graphics: LMA Communications, Natick, MA

Photo credits: © Hulton-Deutsch Collection/Corbis, p. 1; © Ariel Skelley/Corbis, p. 2; © Jose Luis Pelaez, Inc./Corbis, top p. 3; © Don Mason/Corbis, bottom p. 3; © Bettmann/Corbis, left p. 4; © William Coupon/Corbis, right p. 4; © Greg Smith/Corbis SABA, p. 19; © Nassif Jeremie/Corbis SYGMA, p. 27; © Getty Images, p. 33; © George Disario/Corbis, p. 42; © Rob Lewine/Corbis, left p. 54; © Royalty-Free/Corbis, middle p. 54; © Ed Kashi/Corbis, right p. 54; © Norbert Schaefer/Corbis, p. 71; © Jay Dickman/Corbis, p. 72; © Royalty-Free/Corbis, p. 73; © Richard T. Nowitz/Corbis, p. 86; © Jose Luis Pelaez, Inc./Corbis, p. 88; © Pete Saloutos/Corbis, p. 89; © Gabe Palmer/Corbis, p. 90; © Dex Images/Corbis, p. 98; © Peter Turnley/Corbis, p. 99; © Bettmann/Corbis, p. 107; © Royalty-Free/Corbis, top p. 109; © Carl Schneider/Corbis, left p. 109; © Tom & Dee Ann McCarthy/Corbis, p. 110; © Lucidio Studio Inc./Corbis, p. 111; © Jeff Zaruba/Corbis, p. 113; © Smithsonian Institution, p. 127; © Angelo Hornak/Corbis, top p. 129; © Ali Meyer/Corbis, bottom p. 129; © Bettmann/Corbis, p. 130; © Bettmann/Corbis, p. 139; © Royalty-Free/Corbis, from left p. 152; © José Manuel Sanchis Calvete/Corbis, p. 152; © Traudel Sachs/Phototake, p. 152; © Richard List/Corbis, p. 152; © Sukree Sukplang/Reuters/Corbis, p. 152; © Michael Freeman/Corbis, p. 152; © Reuters/Corbis, p. 153; © Royalty-Free/Corbis, left margin p. 152; © Terry and Jerry Lynn, p. 165; © Tony Gentile/Reuters/Corbis, p. 168; © Jack Fields/Corbis, p. 175; © Bettmann/Corbis, p. 176; © Richard Hamilton Smith/Corbis, p. 178; © Alan Schein Photography/Corbis, top p. 179; © Ellis Richard/Corbis, bottom p. 179; © Getty Images, p. 180; © Bettmann/Corbis, p. 187; © ARS/NY, p. 188; © 2005 Artists Rights Society (ARS), New York/ADAGP, Paris, p. 193; © Corbis, p. 199; © David Sailors/Corbis, p. 201; © Shepard Sherbell/Corbis SABA, p. 202; © Farrell Grehan/Corbis, p. 211; © Royalty-Free/Corbis, p. 213; © Ed Bock/Corbis, top left p. 222; © Charles Gupton/Corbis, bottom left p. 224; © Rufus F. Folkks/Corbis, middle p. 222; © Eric Robert/Corbis SYGMA, right p. 222.

For permission to use material from this text or product, submit all requests online at **cengage.com/permissions**
Further permissions questions can be emailed to **permissionrequest@cengage.com**

Library of Congress Control Number: 2003110096

ISBN 13: 978-0-618-23020-4
ISBN 10: 0-618-23020-3

Heinle
20 Channel Center
Boston, MA 02110.

Cengage Learning is a leading provider of customized learning solutions with office locations around the globe, including Singapore, the United Kingdom, Australia, Mexico, Brazil and Japan. Locate your local office at: **international.cengage.com/region**

Cengage Learning products are represented in Canada by Nelson Education, Ltd.

Visit Heinle online at **elt.heinle.com**
Visit our corporate website at **www.cengage.com**

Printed in the United States of America.
3 4 5 6 7 8 9 10   11 10 09

Contents

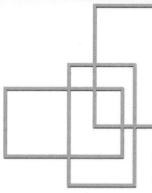

English for Academic Success Series

SERIES EDITORS

Patricia Byrd, Joy M. Reid, Cynthia M. Schuemann

What Is the Purpose of This Series?

The English for Academic Success series is a comprehensive program of student and instructor materials. For students, there are four levels of student language proficiency textbooks in three skill areas (oral communication, reading, and writing), and a supplemental vocabulary textbook at each level. For both instructors and students, a useful website supports classroom teaching, learning, and assessment. In addition, for instructors, there are four Essentials of Teaching Academic Language books (*Essentials of Teaching Academic Oral Communication, Essentials of Teaching Academic Reading, Essentials of Teaching Academic Writing,* and *Essentials of Teaching Academic Vocabulary*). These books provide helpful information for instructors who are new to teaching and for experienced instructors who want to reinforce practices or brush up on current teaching strategies.

The fundamental purpose of the series is to prepare students who are not native speakers of English for academic success in U.S. college degree programs. By studying these materials, students in English for Academic Purposes (EAP) programs will gain the academic language skills they need to learn about the nature and expectations of U.S. college courses.

The series is based on considerable prior research as well as our own investigations of students' needs and interests, instructors' needs and desires, and institutional expectations and requirements. For example, our survey research revealed what problems instructors feel they face in their classrooms and what they actually teach; who the students are and what they know and do not know about the "culture" of U.S. colleges; and what types of exams are required for admission at various colleges.

Student Audience

The materials in this series are for college-bound ESL students at U.S. community colleges and undergraduate programs at other institutions. Some of these students are U.S. high school graduates. Some of them are long-term U.S. residents who graduated from a high school before coming to the United States. Others are newer U.S. residents. Still others are more typical international students. All of them need to develop academic language skills and knowledge of ways to be successful in U.S. college degree courses.

All of the books in this series have been created to implement the English for Academic Success competencies. These competencies are based on those developed by ESL instructors and administrators in Florida, California, and Connecticut to be the underlying structure for EAP courses at colleges in those states. These widely respected competencies assure that the materials meet the real world needs of EAP students and instructors.

All of the books focus on . . .

- Starting where the students are, building on their strengths and prior knowledge (which is considerable, if not always academically relevant), and helping students self-identify needs and plans to strengthen academic language skills
- Academic English, including development of Academic Vocabulary and grammar required by students for academic speaking/listening, reading, and writing
- Master Student Skills, including learning style analysis, strategy training, and learning about the "culture" of U.S. colleges, which lead to their becoming successful students in degree courses and degree programs
- Topics and readings that represent a variety of academic disciplinary areas so that students learn about the language and content of the social sciences, the hard sciences, education, and business as well as the humanities

All of the books provide . . .

- Interesting and valuable content that helps the students develop their knowledge of academic content as well as their language skills and student skills
- A wide variety of practical classroom-tested activities that are easy to teach and engage the students

- Assessment tools at the end of each chapter so that instructors have easy-to-implement ways to assess student learning and students have opportunities to assess their own growth
- Websites for the students and for the instructors: the student sites provide additional opportunities to practice reading, writing, listening, vocabulary development, and grammar. The instructor sites provide instructor's manuals, teaching notes and answer keys, value-added materials like handouts and overheads that can be reproduced to use in class, and assessment tools such as additional tests to use beyond the assessment materials in each book.

What Is the Purpose of the Reading Strand?

The four books in the Reading strand focus on the development of reading skills and general background knowledge necessary for college study. These books are dedicated to meeting the academic needs of ESL students by teaching them how to handle reading demands and expectations of freshman-level classes. The reading selections come from varied disciplines, reflecting courses with high enrollment patterns at U.S. colleges. The passages have been chosen from authentic academic text sources, and are complemented with practical exercises and activities that enhance the teaching-learning process. Students respond positively to being immersed in content from varied disciplines, and vocabulary and skills that are easily recognized as valuable and applicable.

Because of the importance of academic vocabulary in both written and spoken forms, the Reading strand features attention to high-frequency academic words found across disciplines. The books teach students techniques for learning and using new academic vocabulary, both to recognize and understand the words when they read them, and to use important words in their own spoken and written expressions.

In addition to language development, the books provide for content and academic skill development with the inclusion of appropriate academic tasks and by providing strategies to help students better understand and handle what is expected of them in college classes. Chapter objectives specified at the beginning of each chapter include some content area objectives as well as reading and academic skills objectives. For example, student work may include defining key concepts from a reading selection, analyzing the use of facts and examples to support a theory, or paraphrasing information from a reading as they report back on points they have learned. That is, students are not taught to work with the reading selections for some abstract reason, but to learn to make a powerful connection between working with the exercises and activities and success with teacher-assigned tasks from general education disciplines. The chapter objectives are tied to the series competencies which were derived from a review of educator-generated course expectations in community college EAP programs and they reflect a commitment to sound pedagogy.

Each book has a broad "behind-the-scenes" theme to provide an element of sustained content. These themes were selected because of their high interest for students; they are also topics commonly explored in introductory college courses and so provide useful background for students. Materials were selected that are academically appropriate but that do not require expert knowledge by the teacher. The following themes are explored in the Reading strand—Book 1: Society, Book 2: Enduring Issues, Book 3: Diversity, and Book 4: Memory and Learning.

The series also includes a resource book for teachers called *Essentials of Teaching Academic Reading* by Sharon Seymour and Laura Walsh. This practical book provides strategies and activities for the use of instructors new to the teaching of reading and for experienced instructors who want to reinforce their practices or brush up on current teaching strategies.

The website for each book provides additional teaching activities for instructors and study and practice activities for students. These materials include substantial information on practical classroom-based assessment of academic reading to help teachers with the challenging task of analysis of student learning in this area. And, the teacher support on the series website includes printable handouts, quizzes and overhead transparency forms, as well as teaching tips from the authors.

☐ What Is the Organization of *College Reading 1*?

College Reading 1 incorporates intellectually stimulating reading material and language exercises to help low-intermediate level college bound ESL students begin bridging the gap in preparing for academic study.

Themes

Six chapters of readings in psychology, geology, sociology, art, technology, and science present concepts and language that many students will encounter in future courses. The academic disciplines have been chosen to match courses that ESL students most often take in U.S. colleges and universities. The scope of the topics is broad enough to cover a range of interests for students and teachers.

Competencies

College Reading 1 develops the reading competencies listed on page xvii, and referred to as objectives at the start of each chapter. Additional content specific objectives are also listed there. These competencies are developed and reinforced in logical sequence based on reading assignments and hierarchical task complexity.

Reading Development

- Recognizing topics, finding main ideas and supporting details, and recognizing organizational patterns are part of the reading essentials in this book.
- Developing critical thinking skills such as making predictions, drawing conclusions, and contrasting fact vs. opinion are also addressed.

Academic Success

Special feature elements include reading strategy boxes, and Master Student Tips, to highlight important advice for students, and Power Grammar notes to draw attention to grammar shifts that influence meaning. Rather than "grammar in context," *College Reading 1* exploits "grammar from [the] context," of the readings.[1] For example, through reading, students learn to examine parts of speech, explanation or definition markers, and language features that characterize different writing styles found in academic passages.

---

1. Byrd, P. and Reid, J. (1998) *Grammar in the Composition Classroom.* Boston: Heinle.

Content Knowledge

- Three readings per chapter theme facilitate sustained content reading.
- Content skill building is present in every chapter, from learning about heredity and intelligence in Chapter 1 to understanding relationships between art and society in Chapter 2, to analyzing human behaviors in Chapter 4, and to considering questions of ethics and research in Chapter 6.

Vocabulary Development

Vocabulary development is a key feature of *College Reading 1*, so each reading selection was analyzed for its Flesch-Kincaid Grade Level and other factors to ensure that readings were appropriate for this level.

The Web Vocabulary Profiler[2] was used to identify academic[3] and high-frequency[4] vocabulary items in each selection. These analyses aid teachers tremendously in determining which vocabulary items should be stressed in pre- and post-reading activities. *College Reading 1* features a range of vocabulary-building activities aimed at student retention of academic and high-frequency words.

Academic vocabulary words in the reading selections are unobtrusively marked with dotted underlines and a footnoted glossary provides extra help for students when needed.

Chapter Organization and Exercise Types

Each chapter is clearly divided into sections marked Reading Assignment 1, 2, etc. The Reading Assignment sections include common features that indicate prereading, reading, and postreading activities. Following the Reading Assignment sections, each chapter has a final component called Assessing Your Learning at the End of a Chapter.

2. The Web Vocabulary Profiler, maintained by Tom Cobb, analyzes a reading to identify academic and high-frequency vocabulary words within the text. A link to his site can be found by visiting our site at elt.heinle.com/collegereading.
3. *Academic* words refers to the Academic Word List compiled by Dr. Averil Coxhead of Massey University, New Zealand. These 570 word families are commonly found in academic texts from all subjects. A link to her site with the complete list can be found by visiting our website at elt.heinle.com/collegereading.
4. *High-frequency* vocabulary words refer to the 2,000 most frequently used words, the General Service List of English words, also known as the West List (1953).

Getting Ready to Read

Schema-building activities—photographs, group discussions, etc.—activate students' prior knowledge before reading. Students also study potentially unfamiliar vocabulary and key concepts and terms in the academic discipline before they read.

Reading for a Purpose

In this section, readers are guided to read for specific information through prereading tasks such as prediction of ideas, formation of prereading questions responding to short pretest items, and other exercises. These activities focus readers' attention on a particular purpose for reading: finding key ideas.

Demonstrating Comprehension Instead of monotonous comprehension exercises, *College Reading 1* features a variety of interest-peaking activities to monitor comprehension. After each reading, there is not just one or two, but multiple opportunities to assess comprehension. Main idea, major points, supporting ideas, text organization, and confirmation of prereading tests and other activities provide repeated checks of students' understanding of reading.

Questions for Discussion Once students demonstrate a basic understanding of a reading selection, they delve more deeply into its content and language through group and pair discussions. Students write complete sentence answers to the questions after their discussions to exploit the language gained from reading in developing writing skills.

Reading Journal The reading journal feature also facilitates the reading-writing link. Students express reactions to key ideas in reading or write extended answers to discussion questions. Journal writing also serves as another way to check reading comprehension.

Learning Vocabulary Each chapter includes directed vocabulary learning exercises and strategy suggestions for students.

Focusing on (Subject Area) Here students are exposed to more in depth exercise types that focus on content learning expectations or assignments from the different discipline areas associated with each chapter.

Linking Concepts In this section, readers synthesize information gained from two or more sources and transfer ideas from reading to their experiences. Students express these connections in discussion and writing.

Assessing Your Learning at the End of a Chapter

This final section of each chapter asks students to revisit the chapter objectives in a reflective manner, and review for a test. Then, a practice self-test tied to the objectives is provided. Students can test themselves on their understanding and retention of important content and language features in the readings. The items in the student practice tests are similar to items included on the sample tests provided for instructors to use. (Visit the series website at elt.heinle.com/collegereading.) Finally, academic vocabulary from the chapter is also revisited, and a For Further Study web link reminder is provided for students.

Acknowledgments

We would like to thank ESL editor Susan Maguire, who made the project a reality, and developmental editor Kathy Sands Boehmer who kept our large team of at times unwieldy writers on track. Co-series editors Patricia Byrd (Georgia State University), Joy Reid (University of Wyoming), as well as all the team members, lent an enormous store of insight and theoretical and pedagogical knowledge to the series. They were a constant source of support.

We are indebted to our family members who always believed in us. They were there for us whenever the light at the end of the tunnel dimmed.

Also, Steven Donahue, Patricia Killian, and Mary Goodman served us as advisors, and helped guide this book through its early stages. The following reviewers also contributed practical comments and suggestions:

Harriet Allison, Gainesville College
Mark Chalkley, Baltimore City Community College
Mary Corredor, Austin Community College
Amy Drabek, Queens College
Duffy Galda, Pima Community College
Mark Ameen-Johnson, Brooklyn College
Heidi Lamare, Highline Community College
Linda Linn, San Jancinto College
Carole Marquis, Santa Fe Community College
Meredith Massey, Prince George's Community College
Anne-Marie Schlender, Austin Community College
Kent Trickel, Westchester Community College
Colleen Weldele, Palomar College.

Finally, students are the core reason that teachers strive to improve methods and materials. Our students at Miami Dade and Georgia Perimeter Colleges have also greatly influenced our work. Above all, we dedicate these materials to them and wish them success in their academic pursuits.

☐ What Student Competencies Are Covered in *College Reading 1?*

Description of Overall Purposes

Students develop the ability to read text on familiar, basic academic topics with an emphasis on vocabulary expansion and application of critical reading skills.

Materials in this textbook are designed with the following minimum exit objectives in mind:

Competency 1:
(level/global focus)

The student will comprehend texts appropriate to the level on familiar academic topics with emphasis on vocabulary expansion. (Sources include material from secondary textbooks, approximate readability level 6–9)

Competency 2:
(components)

The student will distinguish between main ideas, such as theories to be learned, and supporting information/details/examples in selected texts.

Competency 3:
(organization)

The student will use textual clues to identify simple patterns of organization (e.g., connectors and transitions) to comprehend reading passages appropriate to the level.

Competency 4:
(vocabulary)

The student will develop vocabulary by recognizing context clues and using roots, affixes, definition, restatement, and appositive clues.

Competency 5:
(vocabulary)

The student will develop strategies for discriminating important terminology to be learned for academic purposes such as test-taking, writing, and classroom discussion.

Competency 6:
(critical thinking)

The student will develop the following critical thinking skills when reading. The student will:
a. draw plausible conclusions from stated information.
b. make simple plausible predictions.
c. transfer insights gained from readings to personal experiences.
d. apply content knowledge to academic tasks such as solving problem sets, taking tests, or completing other work that would be required by a discipline instructor, based on subject matter content.

Competency 7:   The student will recognize that the ultimate purpose for
(purpose)   reading for college students is to gain content
                     knowledge for use in other tasks.

Competency 8:   The student will recognize limited cultural references.
(culture)

Competency 9:   The student will enhance English/English dictionary
(dictionary)   skills.

Competency 10: The student will develop an awareness of study skills
(study strategies)   necessary when reading for academic purposes.

▭ What Are the Features of the Reading Books?

The English for Academic Success series is a comprehensive program of student and instructor materials. The fundamental purpose of the program is to prepare students who are not native speakers of English for academic success in U.S. college degree programs.

The Reading strand of the English for Academic Success series focuses on the development of reading skills and general background knowledge. It is dedicated to meeting the academic needs of students by teaching them how to handle the reading demands and expectations of freshman-level college classes. The four books provide reading selections from authentic academic text sources and practical exercises and activities that enhance the teaching-learning process. Students respond positively to being immersed in vocabulary, content, and skills that are easily recognized as valuable and applicable.

Authentic Academic Reading Selections The reading selections come from varied disciplines reflecting freshman-level courses with high enrollment patterns at U.S. colleges. The selections represent true reading demands college students face.

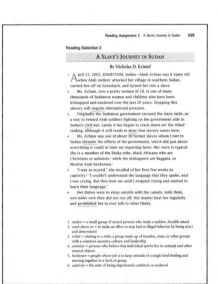

Content and Academic Skill Development In addition to language development, the books provide for content and academic skill development with the inclusion of appropriate academic tasks and by providing strategies to help students better understand and handle what is expected of them in college classes.

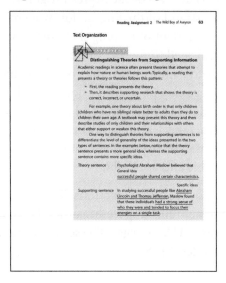

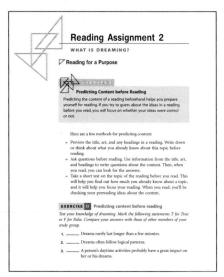

Academic Vocabulary Academic vocabulary is important in both written and spoken forms, so the Reading strand features attention to high-frequency academic words found across disciplines. The books teach students techniques for learning and using new academic vocabulary and provides many practice exercises.

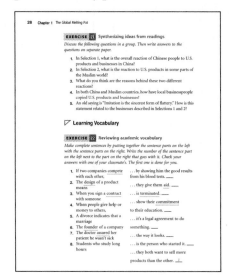

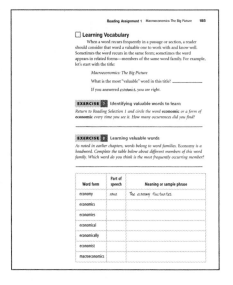

Integrated Review and Assessment Each chapter closes with revisiting objectives and vocabulary and a practice test.

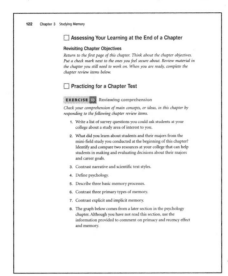

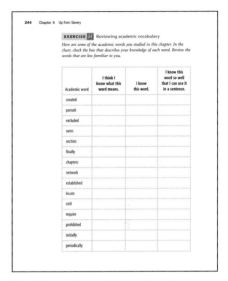

Master Student Tips Master Student Tips throughout the textbooks provide students with short comments on a particular strategy, activity, or practical advice to follow in an academic setting.

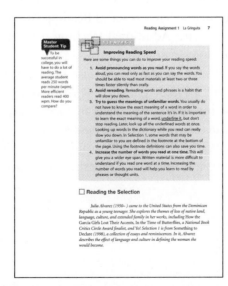

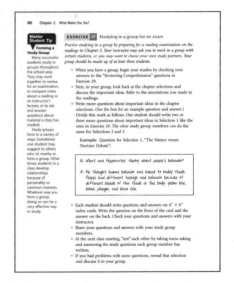

Power Grammar Boxes Students can be very diverse in their grammar and rhetorical needs so each chapter contains Power Grammar boxes that introduce the grammar structures students need to be fluent and accurate in academic English.

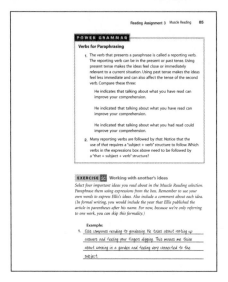

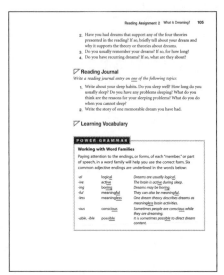

Ancillary Program The following items are available to accompany the English for Academic Success series Reading strand:

- Instructor website: Additional teaching materials, activities, and robust student assessment.
- Student website: Additional exercises and activities.
- The English for Academic Success series Vocabulary books: You can choose the appropriate level to shrinkwrap with your text.
- *The Essentials of Teaching Academic Reading* by Sharon Seymour and Laura Walsh is available for purchase. It gives you theoretical and practical information for teaching oral communication.

Intelligence

ACADEMIC FOCUS: PSYCHOLOGY

Maria Sklodowska-Curie, born in Warsaw, Poland, in 1867, was the first woman scientist to win two Nobel prizes.

Academic Reading Objectives

After completing this chapter, you should be able to:

✓ Check here as you master each objective.

1. Improve reading comprehension and gain content knowledge ☐
2. Understand new academic vocabulary words ☐
3. Use a dictionary to define unfamiliar words ☐
4. Use information about roots and affixes to increase your vocabulary ☐
5. Use diagrams to clarify understanding of concepts ☐
6. Identify reading selection topics ☐

Psychology Objectives

1. Make connections between psychology texts and personal experiences ☐
2. Interpret a table ☐
3. Understand how psychologists use research to reach conclusions ☐
4. Apply a psychological theory to life experiences ☐
5. Remember content using different senses ☐

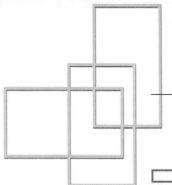

Reading Assignment 1

⬜ Getting Ready to Read

EXERCISE 1 Previewing and discussing key concepts

Discuss the following items, and make lists with your classmates:

1. Reading Selection 1 is from a psychology textbook. What do psychologists study? With your classmates, make a list of things psychologists study.
2. How can you tell if someone is intelligent? Make a list of five characteristics of an intelligent person.
3. Two things that affect intelligence are **heredity** and **environment**. **Heredity** means characteristics a parent gives to her or his or child through genes. Heredity affects eye color, hair color, and height. What are some characteristics you inherited (received through heredity) from your parents? Make a list of the unique physical characteristics you have inherited.

4. **Environment** means the place and things around you. Elements in the environment that can affect your intelligence include the number of books in your house and the school you go to. What other things in your environment can affect intelligence? Make a list of environmental factors that can affect intelligence.

5. Sometimes pictures can help you learn new vocabulary words. Look at the photographs of twins. Read the caption. Discuss the differences with a partner. In your own words, explain the difference between **identical** twins and **fraternal** twins. Do you know anyone who is a twin? Is that person a fraternal or an identical twin?

Identical twins come from the same egg. They share exactly the same genes and so are always the same sex. Fraternal twins come from different eggs. They are like other brothers and sisters. They share half their genes, so they may be the same sex or different sexes.

▭ Reading the Selection

Paying attention to titles and headings can help you understand how information in a reading text is organized. As you read Reading Selection 1 the first time, think about how the information in each section relates to the titles and headings.

While you are reading, you may notice certain words with a dotted underline. These words are in the Academic Word List. You will work with them in later exercises. They are valuable words to know because they are commonly used in most academic disciplines.

Reading Selection 1

INTELLIGENCE

What Is Intelligence?

1   How can you tell if a person is intelligent? You may think: "an intelligent person does well in school." Or "an intelligent person reads a lot." It is not easy to define intelligence. Even psychologists do not agree on its definition. One definition is: intelligence is the ability to learn and adapt to the environment.

2   Psychologists who study intelligence fall into two groups. The first group believes there is one general intelligence. The other group believes there are many kinds of intelligence. They believe people can be intelligent in different ways. The different ways cannot always be measured by intelligence tests. For example, some people can play musical instruments or sing very well. They have musical intelligence.

Albert Einstein

Yoyo Ma

Heredity and Environment

3   Heredity and environment both influence intelligence.

Effects of Heredity

4   Children share physical traits[1] like hair color and eye color with their parents. Through their genes, parents pass some traits to their children. This is called heredity. Most psychologists believe intelligence is inherited (passed from parents to children). The way genes affect intelligence is complex. For example, there is no single gene for height. Similarly, there is no single gene for intelligence. Many genes affect intelligence.

5   Researchers try to understand how heredity and environment influence intelligence. One way to do this is using twin and adoption studies. Studying twins helps researchers understand how genes influence intelligence. Identical twins inherit the exact same genes from their parents. Fraternal twins are like brothers and sisters. They share half of the same genes.

Effects of Environment

6   The effects of environment on intelligence are divided into **two** categories:

1. **Shared Environment.** Your shared environment influences[2] you and your brothers and sisters. You all came from the same family, so you share the same environment. In your family, the economic status if you are rich or poor—is the same for each child. Also, the level of your parents' education is the same.

2. **Non-shared Environment.** Some things about your environment are unique. They are not shared with your brothers and sisters. For example, how much attention you received from your parents can be different from your brothers and sisters. Your friends, your experiences, activities, and education are also different. These are examples of non-shared environment.

---

1. **trait** (trāt) *n.* Characteristic; feature.
2. **in•flu•ence** (ĭn′floo-əns) *tr. v.* Has an effect on.

Twin Studies

7   There are **two** kinds of twins:

1. **Identical Twins.** These twins develop from a single egg. They are both the same sex. They have exactly the same genes.
2. **Fraternal Twins.** These are as different as any brothers or sisters. They develop from different eggs. They can be the same sex, or they can be of opposite sexes.

8   Researchers[3] interested in intelligence study twins. Identical twins who are adopted[4] at birth by different people have similar intelligence. Fraternal twins who are raised together do not always have similar intelligence. This shows that intelligence is influenced more by genes than shared environment. From these studies, researchers conclude that genes are important to intelligence. However, shared environment does not appear to be important at all.

Source: Adapted from *Introduction to Psychology*, (2001). Elgin, IL: McDougal Littell, pp. 158–159.

3. **re•search•er** (rĭ-sûrch´ər) *n.* Person who conducts scholarly or scientific investigations or inquiries.
4. **a•dopt•ed** (ə-dŏpt´-ed) *adj.* Taken into one's family through legal means and raised as one's own child.

▭ Assessing Your Learning: Intelligence

Demonstrating Comprehension

EXERCISE 2 **Remembering with headings**

Write the information you remember from each section under these headings. Write without looking back at the reading selection. The first one is done for you as an example.

1. "What Is Intelligence?"

   Intelligence is the ability to learn and adapt to the

   environment.

2. "Effects of Heredity"

   _____

   _____

   _____

3. "Effects of Environment"

   _____

   _____

   _____

4. "Twin Studies"

   _____

   _____

   _____

Now compare what you remember with a partner's. Add any details you forgot.

EXERCISE 3   Checking comprehension

Read the following statements. If the statement is true, write T. If the statement is false, write F and change the statement to make it true. The first one has been done for you as an example.

                            disagree

1. __f__ ~~All~~ psychologists ~~agree~~ on the definition of intelligence.

2. _____ Psychologists who study intelligence can be sorted into two different groups.

3. _____ Identical twins, like brothers and sisters, share half the same genes.

4. _____ Twin studies help psychologists understand how intelligence is related to genes.

5. _____ Heredity and environment both affect intelligence.

6. _____ Heredity and environment both affect physical traits.

7. _____ A family is an example of a shared environment.

8. _____ Adoption studies help researchers understand the relationship between heredity and intelligence.

9. _____ All children in a family receive the same amount of attention from their parents.

10. _____ Environment is not as important as heredity in intelligence.

11. _____ Identical twins cannot be of different sexes.

12. _____ There are various ways people can be intelligent.

13. _____ Parents pass many genes to their children.

☐ Learning Vocabulary

STRATEGY

Academic Word List

Researchers have found that certain words appear over and over again in academic readings. These same words appear across academic disciplines, from textbooks in psychology and world history to articles on business and computer science. They are important words to learn and to remember. Common academic words in the reading selections in this textbook are marked with dotted underlines. You may already know some of these words, but others may be new. Develop a system for recording new words and definitions so that you can study and remember them. Make learning unfamiliar vocabulary a priority, and you will not only expand your vocabulary but also perform better in academic courses.

EXERCISE 4   **Studying academic vocabulary**

Academic vocabulary words are words from the reading selection that are commonly found in academic textbooks. Study the list of words below from Reading Selection 1, and then learn them by following these guidelines:

1. *Number a paper from 1 to 21. Copy these words, leaving space for a definition. The parentheses number after each word is the number of the paragraph where the word is found.*
2. *Write a definition, synonym, or translation for the words you already know.*
3. *Compare your list with a partner's. Help each other learn new words.*
4. *Share your list with your classmates. Your teacher can help you define the words you do not know.*

1. intelligence (¶ 1)
2. ability (¶ 1)
3. adapt (¶ 1)
4. environment (¶ 1)
5. general (¶ 2)
6. measure (¶ 2)
7. musical (¶ 2)
8. physical (¶ 3)
9. affect (¶ 3)
10. height (¶ 3)
11. adopt (¶ 4)
12. exact (¶ 4)
13. effect (¶ 5)
14. divide (¶ 5)
15. economic (¶ 5)
16. unique (¶ 5)
17. attention (¶ 5)
18. experience (¶ 5)
19. activity (¶ 5)
20. opposite (¶ 6)
21. conclude (¶ 7)

EXERCISE 5 Completing a word puzzle

Using the clues on the next page, complete the word puzzle with academic words.

1.							I							
2.							N							
3.							T							
4.							E							
5.							L							
6.							L							
7.							I							
8.							G							
9.							E							
10.							N							
11.							C							
12.							E							

Clues

1. Things around you
2. Related to money
3. Get used to, adjust
4. An event that you can learn from
5. Something you are able to do; a talent
6. Strong; important
7. Related to the body, not mental
8. Not specific
9. To influence
10. One of its kind
11. Make a decision based on evidence
12. Result

POWER GRAMMAR

Some words have similar **roots** but are used in different forms. Roots are the base form of a word. For example, here are three different forms of the word *intelligent* and three for the word *influence*:

> She is **intelligent**.

> Psychologists study **intelligence**.

> They solved the problem **intelligently**.

> Parents **influence** their children.

> **Influential** people came to see us today.

> My **influence** at this school is not important.

When learning new words, try to learn all common forms of the word.

EXERCISE 6 **Studying word families**

Here are some words with similar roots from Reading Selection 1. Complete the chart by writing the base word and its meaning. The first one has been done for you as an example.

Noun	Verb	Adjective	Adverb	Base Word	Meaning
1. ability				*able*	*can, talented, capable*
2. adoption	adopt	adopted; adoptable			
3. belief	believe	believable	believably		
4.		exact; exacting	exactly		
5. genes, genetics		genetic	genetically		
6.		general	generally		
7. height		high	highly		
8. heredity	inherit	inherited			
9. influence	influence	influential	influentially		
10. music, musician		musical	musically		
11.		physical	physically		
12. power	power	powerful	powerfully		
13. psychologists, psychology		psychological	psychologically		

EXERCISE 7 **Using the correct form**

Complete the following sentences with the correct word form from the chart on page 12.

1. He has the _____ to go to college.

2. _____ studies explain how genetics affects intelligence.

3. Some psychologists _____ that your intelligence comes from your parents.

4. Their theories are _____.

5. Identical twins have an _____ match of genes.

6. Hair color is one characteristic determined by your _____.

7. It is _____ easy to tell the difference between fraternal twins.

8. What is your _____?

9. Nathan _____ his green eyes from his mother.

10. Shared environment does not have a great _____ on intelligence.

11. Einstein's work has been _____.

12. Mozart had _____ talent.

13. Eye and hair color are examples of _____ characteristics.

14. It is a _____ car.

15. _____ are people who study differences in intelligence.

EXERCISE 8 **Using a dictionary with confusing word pairs**

Some English words are confusing because they look very similar. Here are some examples. Find these words in a dictionary. Write a definition for each one. Then write a sentence using each word correctly. Share your definitions and sentences with your classmates.

1. adapt

Definition: _____

_____

Sentence: _____

_____

2. adopt

Definition: _____

_____

Sentence: _____

_____

3. effect

Definition: _____

_____

Sentence: _____

_____

4. affect

Definition: _____

_____

Sentence: _____

_____

▭ **Focusing on Psychology**

Psychologists study human behavior in a scientific way. First, they make a hypothesis, or guess, about how humans act. Then, they check their guess by observing and testing people. Good readers not only try to understand a text but also compare what they read with their experiences. Think like a psychologist.

Answer the following questions. Base your answers on your experiences.

- You and your brothers and sisters have the same shared environment. Are you similar to or different from your brothers and sisters in intelligence?

- Does your experience support what psychologists say about shared environment? (If you do not have a brother or sister, base your answer to this question on brothers or sisters you know.)

Of course, psychologists do not base a hypothesis on the experiences of one or two people. The more people who can provide information, the more accurate the hypothesis will be.

EXERCISE 9   **Checking a theory by gathering samples**

Make a chart like this one for all the people in your class. (Students with more than one brother or sister will have more than one answer.) What hypothesis can you make from your results?

		Check One (✔)		
Name	**Brother or sister's name**	**More intelligent**	**Less intelligent**	**About the same**

▭ Questions for Review

EXERCISE 10   **Reflecting on new learning**

Work with a group of three or four other students. Discuss these questions:

1. What do you think are the positives and negatives of being a twin? Give examples to support your opinion.
2. Review the list of characteristics of intelligence you made before you read this selection. Would you add anything new to the list now?

▭ Linking Concepts

Master Student Tip

▼ Keeping a reading journal can help you as you learn. You can record your thoughts about what you read.

EXERCISE 11   **Writing in your reading journal**

Answer the following questions in a journal. Your instructor may respond to ideas you include in your journal.

1. Write your personal answer to one of the discussion topics in Exercise 10.
2. Why is intelligence so important?
3. Describe the most intelligent person you have ever met.
4. What else would you like to know about intelligence?

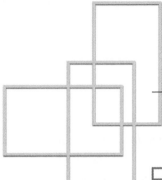

Reading Assignment 2

RESEARCH ON INTELLIGENCE

🖵 Getting Ready to Read

EXERCISE 12 **Thinking about verbs**

In academic textbooks, some common verbs are used to explain the results of research studies. Some of these verbs are listed below.

Match each verb with its meaning.

As you read, find these verbs and circle them.

_____ review	**1.** connect; relate
_____ influence	**2.** tell; give the results
_____ claim	**3.** look at again; go over
_____ link	**4.** guess about the future
_____ predict	**5.** declare; argue
_____ report	**6.** affect; change
_____ develop	**7.** fill out
_____ test	**8.** use mind to gain knowledge
_____ complete	**9.** produce
_____ study	**10.** examine, assess

▭ Reading the Selection

EXERCISE **13**   Discovering preconceptions

Before you read Selection 2, fill in the left side of the following chart to tell if you agree or disagree with the statements. Explain why you agree or disagree. After you read the selection, complete the right side of the chart. See if your answers have changed.

	Before you read	**After you read**
	Agree or disagree	**Agree or disagree**
1. Going to school has a positive effect on intelligence.		
Why?		
2. Men are more intelligent than women.		
Why?		
3. Genes influence intelligence.		
Why?		

Reading Selection 2

RESEARCH ON INTELLIGENCE

1   In 1996, the American Psychological Association reviewed different studies about intelligence. Here is a summary of those studies:

- Heredity influences intelligence. However, we do not know how genes influence intelligence.
- Going to school is important to the development of intelligence. However, we do not know what parts of schooling are important for intelligence.
- There are no important differences between men and women in intelligence. However, there are some differences in specific abilities. Men usually score higher on math skills, and women on verbal skills.
- Intelligence tests can predict success in school. They can predict high grades. They can also predict the number of years of education a person will complete.
- Intelligence tests do not give information about all types of intelligence. They do not tell us about creativity, wisdom, and sensitivity.

2   Researchers continue to study the role of genes in intelligence. In May 1998, Robert Plomin reported the discovery of a gene that is linked to high intelligence. Reports in September 1999 claimed that scientists changed a gene in mice to make them more intelligent. Genes are not the whole answer to the question of what makes us intelligent. More research will tell us more about intelligence.

Source: Adapted from *Introduction to Psychology*, (2001). Elgin, IL: McDougal Littell, pp. 159–160.

▭ Assessing Your Learning: Research on Intelligence

Demonstrating Comprehension

EXERCISE 14   Revisiting preconceptions

Complete the right half of the chart in Exercise 13. Have you changed any of your opinions? Explain why you agree or disagree with the psychologists' research conclusions.

EXERCISE 15   Restating conclusions and discoveries

Respond to the following items.

1. Restate five conclusions the American Psychological Association made from its review of the intelligence studies. Restate the conclusions in your own words.

   a. _Genes influence intelligence._

   b. _____

   c. _____

   d. _____

   e. _____

2. What did Robert Plomin discover about the role of genes in intelligence?

   _____

   _____

   _____

3. How did scientists make mice more intelligent?

   _____

   _____

   _____

☐ Focusing on Psychology

EXERCISE 16   **Experimenting and comparing**

Answer these questions.

1. The speed limit is fifty-five miles per hour. How far will you go in one hour? Two hours? Three hours? How long will it take to go five hundred miles?
2. In thirty seconds, write the names of as many types of jobs as you can think of in which the person doing the job usually wears a uniform.
3. Which was easier to answer—question 1 or question 2?
4. Do you agree with this statement from the reading selection: "Men usually score higher on math skills, and women on verbal skills"?
5. Make a list of the students in your class. Ask each student which question was easier to answer—question 1 or question 2. Decide if the information you gathered from your classmates confirms or disagrees with what psychologists say about the difference between men and women.

☐ Learning Vocabulary

Master Student Tip

▼ One way to find out the meanings of words is to ask other people. Here are some ways you can ask about vocabulary words:

▪ What does _____ mean?
▪ What is the meaning of _____?
▪ Could you please use that word in a sentence.

EXERCISE 17   **Reviewing academic vocabulary**

These words from Reading Selection 2 are commonly found in academic textbooks. You learned the meaning of some of these words in the "Getting Ready to Read" activity before the reading selection. Put a check mark (✔) next to the verbs you studied already.

1. influence
2. claim
3. discovery
4. link
5. predict
6. report
7. sensitivity
8. wisdom

EXERCISE 18   **Asking about vocabulary and taking notes**

In your notebook or reading journal, write the words from the list above that you do not know. Ask your instructor or another native speaker of English what those words mean. Listen carefully, and write the meanings of the words in your notebook.

STRATEGY

Collocation

Many times, English words are grouped together in phrases. You can improve your vocabulary by remembering not only words but also the other words that are commonly found before or after the word.

EXERCISE 19 **Studying collocation**

Study the word boxes below. Write a sentence for each group of words.
The first ones have been done for you as examples.

claim	**1.** to be **2.** to have **3.** that
discovery	**4.** of **5.** on **6.** that
link	**7.** between **8.** to **9.** up with **10.** with
sensitivity	**11.** to **12.** toward

Example

1. *They claim to be intelligent.*

    They claim to have the right answer.

2. _____

_____

3. _____

_____

4. _____

_____

5. _____

_____

6. _____

_____

7. _____

_____

8. _____

_____

9. _____

_____

10. _____

_____

11. _____

_____

12. _____

_____

⬜ Questions for Review

EXERCISE 20   **Discussing with classmates**

Discuss the following questions in small groups.

1. What do you think causes men to score higher on math skills, and women on verbal skills, on intelligence tests?
2. At the end of Reading Selection 2 is this sentence: "Reports in September 1999 claimed that scientists changed a gene in mice to make them more intelligent." Imagine if scientists could change a gene in humans to make them more intelligent. With your group members, make a list of the positive and negative effects of making people more intelligent.

Positive Effects	Negative Effects

⬜ Linking Concepts

EXERCISE 21   **Writing in your reading journal**

Write responses to the following items in your reading journal.

1. Write about any of the discussion topics from the exercise above.
2. In your own words, define **creativity**, **wisdom**, or **sensitivity**. Describe a person you know who exemplifies one of those characteristics.
3. Explain how **creativity**, **wisdom**, or **sensitivity** is different from **intelligence**.

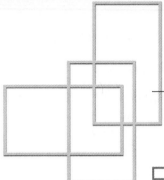

Reading Assignment 3

APPROACHES TO UNDERSTANDING INTELLIGENCE

▢ Getting Ready to Read

EXERCISE 22 Completing a survey

Make a check mark by the activities you are good at.

1. _____ Explaining difficult ideas to other people

2. _____ Solving math problems

3. _____ Imagining beforehand how things should be arranged before you move them

4. _____ Singing or playing music

5. _____ Understanding how other people feel

6. _____ Sports or dancing

7. _____ Recognizing and classifying different types of plants and animals

Review the list above. Which of those activities do think require intelligence? Discuss your choices with your classmates.

▢ Reading the Selection

Experts usually have the best information. However, sometimes experts disagree. Then you have to look at the evidence that supports different experts' opinions and decide which expert to believe. Reading Selection 3 explains two different expert opinions on intelligence.

EXERCISE 23 Comparing the opinions of experts

After you read Selection 3, go back and fill in the diagram with the evidence that supports each opinion. Think about the evidence. Explain which opinion you agree with and why. The first one has been done for you as an example.

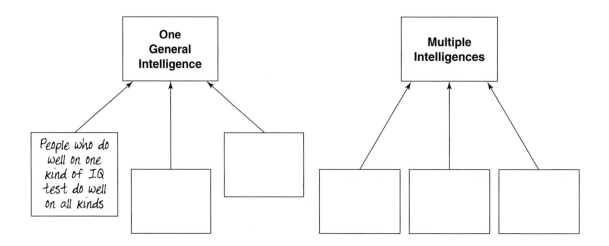

One General Intelligence

People who do well on one kind of IQ test do well on all kinds

Multiple Intelligences

Reading Selection 3

APPROACHES TO UNDERSTANDING INTELLIGENCE

1 It pays to be smart, but we are not all smart in the same way. You may know every baseball score over the past five years for your home team, but may be only average at math. You may be a talented[1] musician, but you might not be a good reader. Each of us is different.

2 Psychologists <u>disagree</u> about what is intelligence and what are talents or personal abilities. Psychologists have two different views on intelligence. Some believe there is one general intelligence. Others believe there are many different intelligences.

---

1. **tal•ent•ed** (tăl′ənt-ĭd) *adj.* Gifted, able, very good.

One General Intelligence

3   Some psychologists say there is one type of intelligence that can be measured with IQ tests.[2] These psychologists support their view with research that concludes that people who do well on one kind of test for mental ability do well on other tests. They do well on tests using words, numbers, or pictures. They do well on individual or group tests, and written or oral tests. Those who do poorly on one test, do the same on all tests.

Speed and Effectiveness

4   Studies of the brain show that there is a biological basis for general intelligence. The brains of intelligent people use less energy during problem solving. The brain waves[3] of people with higher intelligence show a quicker reaction. Some researchers conclude that differences in intelligence result from differences in the speed and effectiveness of information processing by the brain.

Howard Gardner

Gardner's Theory of Multiple Intelligences

5   There is an old saying about psychologists: when a psychologist has one child, all children are alike; when he or she has two children, the world is divided into two kinds of people: extroverts[4] and introverts,[5] masculine and feminine. But when a psychologist has three children, all children are different.

2. **I•Q tests** = Tests that measure intelligence; *IQ* stands for intelligence quotient.
3. **brain wave** (brān wāv) *n.* Electric activity of the brain.
4. **ex•tro•vert** (ĕk´strə-vûrt´) *n.* Outgoing person.
5. **in•tro•vert** (ĭn´trə-vûrt´) *n.* Shy, quiet person.

6   Howard Gardner, a psychologist at the Harvard School of Education, has four children. He believes that all children are different. He thinks children shouldn't be tested by one intelligence test. He believes general intelligence exists. However, he doesn't think it tells much about the talents of a person outside of formal schooling. He believes that the human mind has different intelligences. These intelligences allow us to solve the kinds of problems we are presented with in life. Each of us has different abilities within these intelligences. Gardner believes that the purpose of school should be to encourage development of all of our intelligences.

7   Gardner says that his theory is based in biology. For example, when one part of the brain is injured, other parts of the brain still work. People who cannot talk because of brain damage can still sing. So, there is not just one intelligence to lose. Gardner has identified 8 different kinds of intelligence, linguistic, mathematical, spatial, musical, interpersonal, intrapersonal, body-kinesthetic, and naturalistic. This table describes Gardner's 8 different kinds of intelligence.

Gardener's eight intelligences		
Intelligence	**Description**	**Examples in people**
1. Linguistic intelligence	using language; expressing yourself and understanding people	poets, writers, editors, journalists, speakers, lawyers
2. Mathematical intelligence	using numbers; reasoning well, understanding principles	mathematicians, scientists, economists, computer programmers
3. Spatial intelligence	forming a mental model in space	navigators, chess players, architects, sculptors, cartoonists, hairdressers

Gardener's eight intelligences (cont.)		
Intelligence	**Description**	**Examples in people**
4. Musical intelligence	thinking musically: hearing and recognizing patterns; creating music	musicians, composers
5. Interpersonal intelligence	understanding other people, and their feelings, knowing how to communicate and work in groups	group members, leaders, teachers, counselors
6. Intrapersonal intelligence	understanding yourself—who you are, and what you can and and can't do	useful in any job
7. Body-kinesthetic intelligence	using your whole body or parts of your body to solve problems, making something, or act out something	athletes, dancers and actors
8. Naturalistic intelligence	recognizing and classifying landforms and bodies of water, plants, minerals, and animals	mapmakers, farmers, hunters, botanists, chefs, geologist, biologist

Source: Adapted from *Introduction to Psychology*, (2001). Elgin, IL: McDougal Littell, pp. 154–164.

☐ Assessing Your Learning: Approaches to Understanding Intelligence

Demonstrating Comprehension

EXERCISE 24 **Answering multiple-choice questions**

Answer the following questions about Reading Selection 3:

1. Psychologists

   a. agree about intelligence.

   b. disagree about intelligence.

   c. all believe there is one general intelligence.

   d. all believe there are multiple intelligences.

2. Which of the following provides the evidence for one general intelligence?

   a. People who do well on one kind of intelligence test do well on other tests.

   b. Most intelligent people do well on some intelligence tests.

   c. Intelligent people do not do well on group tests.

   d. Intelligent people do better on written tests than on oral tests.

3. Howard Gardner has

   a. one child.

   b. two children.

   c. three children.

   d. four children.

4. Which of the following does Howard Gardner believe?

   a. All children are alike.

   b. Children should be tested by one intelligence test.

   c. There is no general intelligence.

   d. Children have different intelligences.

5. According to Gardner, schools would be better if they spent more time

   a. testing students' IQs.

   b. teaching what students do best, and forget about trying to improve general intelligence.

   c. encouraging the development of all intelligences.

   d. focusing on finding the most intelligent students.

6. Michael Jordan probably has high

   a. spatial intelligence.

   b. body-kinesthetic intelligence.

   c. linguistic intelligence.

   d. naturalistic intelligence.

7. A good salesperson has to communicate with people in order to sell things. A good salesperson would probably have

   a. intrapersonal intelligence.

   b. spatial intelligence.

   c. interpersonal intelligence.

   d. musical intelligence.

8. Which of these people use spatial intelligence in their jobs?

   a. Cooks

   b. Judges

   c. Businesspeople

   d. Artists

STRATEGY

Topics

A topic is the name, theme, or general subject of a piece of writing. It tells what the writing is about. Recognizing the topic helps you find out the main idea of a passage. A topic is not a complete sentence. It is usually written at the beginning of a passage or section as a title or heading.

EXERCISE 25   **Locating topics in titles**

Each reading selection in this chapter has a title to help readers anticipate what the passage is about and focus on a main idea. As you read a title, ask yourself, What is this passage about? Write the title of each selection, and then explain the topic in your own words.

1. Reading Selection 1: *Intelligence*

    Explanation: *The author defines intelligence.*

2. Reading Selection 2: _____

    Explanation: _____

3. Reading Selection 3: _____

    Explanation: _____

Notice how each of these titles includes a noun: intelligence, research, *and* approaches. *The noun is the general idea.*

EXERCISE 26   **Recognizing topics**

*Look at the following phrases and decide if each one is a possible title or not. Write T for Topic or N for No in the blank spaces. Remember that a noun is required and that it needs to be a **general idea**.*

1. _____ Effects and Heredity   6. _____ Can Predict

2. _____ Through Their Genes   7. _____ In the Same Way

3. _____ Does Well   8. _____ One General Intelligence

4. _____ Twin Studies   9. _____ Schooling

5. _____ Influences on Heredity   10. _____ Gardner's Theory

▭ Focusing on Psychology

EXERCISE 27   Recognizing different intelligences

What kind of intelligence do you have? Try this activity. First, answer each question about you. Then, stand up and walk around the class. Ask each classmate which of the following activities he or she can do. Ask him or her to show you. Find out what kind of intelligence your classmates have.

Verbal/Linguistic

Can you . . .

1. recite four lines from a poem? Answer: Yes or No. If you answered Yes, be prepared to recite the poem.

2. name five words that include the word *corn* as part of a larger word (for example, *corner*)?

Logical/Mathematical

Can you . . .

3. complete this sequence of numbers and explain the logic?

   4 9 16 25 _____

4. categorize the following items in any way that can be justified? Form at least three categories, include at least three items in each category, and use each item once.

eyeglasses	roses	sweater	paintbrush	snow
orange juice	dictionary	scissors	typewriter	gardenias
perfume	clouds	button	pen	sewing machine

Visual/Spatial

Can you . . .

5. select one of the following abstract terms and draw it?

sensitivity   wisdom   creativity   intelligence

6. name as many things as possible that you see in the inkblot?

Musical/Rhythmic

Can you . . .

7. whistle a song?
8. explain 6/8 time signature in music?

Interpersonal

Can you . . .

9. convince someone to try one of these tasks that the person doesn't believe he or she can do?
10. collaborate with someone else in this class to write a poem about students?

Intrapersonal

Can you . . .

11. draw an animal that is most like you and then explain the reason or resemblance between you and that animal?
12. explain to someone else how you have coped with a difficulty in your life?

Bodily/Kinesthetic

Can you . . .

13. use your body to make the letters of your name?
14. stand on one foot with your eyes closed for five seconds?

Naturalistic Intelligence

Can you . . .

15. explain why clouds that bring rain look different from clouds that do not bring rain?
16. explain how you know house cats and lions are related?

▭ Learning Vocabulary

EXERCISE 28   Reviewing academic vocabulary

These words from the reading selection are commonly found in academic textbooks. Study the list of words below, and then learn them by following these guidelines.

1. Number a paper from 1 to 18. Copy these words, leaving space for a definition. The paragraph location is in parentheses next to the word.
2. Write a definition, synonym, or translation for the words you already know.
3. Compare your list with a partner's. Help each other learn new words.
4. Share your list with your classmates. Your instructor can help you define the words you do not know.

1. disagree (¶ 1)	10. damage (¶ 7 chart)
2. mental (¶ 3)	11. editors (¶ 7 chart)
3. basis (¶ 4)	12. principles (¶ 7 chart)
4. energy (¶ 4)	13. economists (¶ 7 chart)
5. problem solving (¶ 4)	14. computer (¶ 7 chart)
6. brain waves (¶ 4)	15. spatial (¶ 7 chart)
7. formal schooling (¶ 6)	16. creating (¶ 7 chart)
8. encourage (¶ 6)	17. communicate (¶ 7 chart)
9. development (¶ 6)	18. job (¶ 7 chart)

EXERCISE 29   Learning more about words

One way to learn about words is to put them into groups by meaning. Work with a partner to put the words listed above into categories by meaning. Explain them.

Example

mental, problem solving, brain waves, and creating are related because they have to do with the mind.

POWER GRAMMAR

Affixes

Affixes are word parts that go together to build words. If you know the meanings of the affixes, you can sometimes guess the meanings of words. Suffixes are affixes that come at the end of a word.

Look at these words: *farmer, actor, scientist, musician*
What do these affixes mean? *-er, -or, -ist, -ian*
All of these mean a person who does something.

A farm*er* is a person who farms. An act*or* is a person who acts. A scient*ist* is a person who does scientific experiments. A musi*cian* is a person who plays or sings music.

EXERCISE 30   **Writing affixes**

Use the list of "examples in people" from the chart at the end of Reading Selection 3 (pp. 28 and 29). Write the examples under the appropriate list:

-er	-or	-ist	-ian
1. Writer	1.	1.	1.
2.	2.	2.	2.
3.	3.	3.	
4.	4.	4.	
5.	5.	5.	
6.		6.	
7.		7.	
8.			
9.			

	-er	-or	-ist	-ian
10.				
11.				
12.				
13.				

☐ Questions for Review

EXERCISE **31**   **Participating in small-group discussion**

Work with a group of three or four classmates. Nominate a group secretary or recorder to write down information. Discuss the following items:

1. For each occupation you filled in above, discuss what type of intelligence(s) a person should have to do that job well.

   Example

   Writers need to have linguistic intelligence.

2. What could schools do to teach all types of intelligence? Make a list of Gardner's eight types of intelligence. Beside each type of intelligence, write an activity that teachers could use to help children with that type of intelligence.

   Example

   Linguistic: Teachers could have their students give presentations.

▭ Linking Concepts

EXERCISE 32   **Using different senses to help memory**

Often when you read something, your instructor will ask you to remember what you read. Here are two ways to remember Gardner's intelligences. Practice each one.

   A. One way to remember new ideas is by "seeing them in your mind." Follow these steps to help you remember each type of intelligence:
      1. Look again at the intelligences chart at the end of Reading Selection 3.
      2. Notice that each kind of intelligence has a little picture. Look at the picture.
      3. Close your eyes and see the picture in your mind.
      4. Relate the picture and the type of intelligence.
      5. Try to remember each of the eight types of intelligences.
      6. Tell a partner what you remember.

   B. Another way to remember important content is to relate actions to ideas. Follow these steps to help you remember each type of intelligence:
      1. Look at the chart again.
      2. Remember the activities you did related to each type of intelligence.
      3. Think of the activities and say the name of the intelligences.
      4. Tell a partner what you remember.

   Can you remember all eight of Gardner's intelligences now?

EXERCISE 33   **Writing in your reading journal**

Write about one of these topics in your reading journal.

   1. Write about your experience trying to learn Gardner's eight types of intelligences by "seeing" pictures in your mind or associating concepts with activities. Which method works better for you?
   2. Review the chart of Gardner's intelligences. What kind of intelligences do you think you have? Write about one thing you can do that shows you have that kind of intelligence.
   3. Do you wish you were stronger in one kind of intelligence? Write about what you wish you were stronger in and why.

⬜ Assessing Your Learning at the End of the Chapter: Revisiting Objectives

Return to the first page of this chapter. Think about the chapter objectives. Put a check mark next to the objectives you feel confident about. Review the material in the chapter you need to learn better. When you are ready, take the practice test in Exercise 34. These items reflect the chapter objectives and come from all three reading selections.

EXERCISE 34 Reviewing comprehension

Check your comprehension of important material in this chapter by answering these questions. First, write notes to answer the questions without looking back. Then, use the readings and exercises to check your answers and revise them. Write your final answers in complete sentences on separate paper.

Practicing for a Chapter Test

1. What is the difference between identical and fraternal twins?
2. Why do psychologists study twins?
3. What is heredity?
4. What is one thing researchers have found out about intelligence?
5. What are Gardner's eight intelligences?
6. Explain the difference between *adapt* and *adopt*.
7. Do you agree or disagree with the following statements? Base your answers on your personal life experiences. Give specific examples from your life or the life of someone you know to support your answers.
   a. "Heredity affects intelligence."
   b. "Women have stronger verbal intelligence than men."
   c. "People who don't do well on traditional intelligence tests may be intelligent in other areas."

▭ Academic Vocabulary Review

Here are some academic vocabulary words that were introduced in this chapter. Confirm the words whose meanings you know. Identify the words that are not yet part of your active vocabulary. Relearn the words you need to relearn.

1. ability	11. computer	21. editor	31. influence	41. predict
2. activity	12. conclude	22. effect	32. intelligence	42. principles
3. adapt	13. creating	23. encourage	33. job	43. problem solving
4. adopt	14. damage	24. energy	34. link	44. report
5. affect	15. development	25. environment	35. measure	45. sensitivity
6. attention	16. disagree	26. exact	36. mental	46. spatial
7. basis	17. discovery	27. experience	37. musical	47. theories
8. brain wave	18. divide	28. formal schooling	38. opposite	48. unique
9. claim	19. economic	29. general	39. physical	49. wisdom
10. communicate	20. economists	30. height	40. powerful	

WEB POWER

You will find additional exercises related to the content in this chapter at **elt.heinle.com/collegereading.**

Answer key for the puzzle

1.				E	N	V	**I**	R	O	N	M	E	N	T
2.				E	C	O	**N**	O	M	I	C
3.			A	D	A	P	**T**
4.				E	X	P	**E**	R	I	E	N	C	E
5.				A	B	I	**L**	I	T	Y
6.	P	O	W	E	R	F	U	**L**
7.				P	H	Y	S	**I**	C	A	L
8.								**G**	E	N	E	R	A	L
9.				A	F	F	**E**	C	T
10.					U	N	**I**	Q	U	E
11.				C	O	N	**C**	L	U	D	E
12.				E	F	F	**E**	C	T

Thinking Critically about the Internet

ACADEMIC FOCUS:
COMPUTERS/INFORMATION TECHNOLOGY

Academic Reading Objectives

After completing this chapter,
you should be able to:

✓ Check here as you
master each objective.

1. Understand new academic vocabulary words ☐
2. Identify main ideas of paragraphs and reading
   selections ☐
3. Analyze the difference between fact and opinion ☐
4. Identify word prefixes that make opposites ☐
5. Identify words that signal examples ☐
6. Use a dictionary to look up words with multiple
   meanings ☐

Computer/Information Technology Objectives

1. Identify fact and opinion on an Internet website ☐
2. Discuss positive and negative influences of
   technology ☐
3. Understand how technology has influenced
   history ☐
4. Participate in a chat group or send an e-mail that
   shows understanding of electronic etiquette ☐
5. Evaluate the results of an Internet search ☐

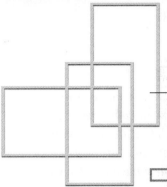

Reading Assignment 1

▭ Getting Ready to Read

EXERCISE **1** Participating in class discussion

Discuss the following questions with your classmates:

1. What is the Internet?

   The Internet is...

2. What are some ways people use the Internet? Think of as many examples as you can.

   People use the Internet for...

3. How do you use the Internet for school? Think of as many examples as you can.

   At school I use the Internet to...

4. Share examples of inappropriate uses of the Internet.

   Some examples of inappropiate uses are...

5. The title of Reading Selection 1 is "Thinking Critically about the Internet." What kinds of things should people think about when they find information on the Internet?

   They should think about...

6. Why should they think about these things?

   They should think about these things because...

7. Talk about a recent time when you used the Internet. How was your experience?

   I used the Internet...

EXERCISE **2**   **Previewing technology vocabulary**

When people invent new technology, they have to give it a name. Many times, it is easy to "borrow" a word that people know already. People can also create new words by combining existing words. Here are some words borrowed or created by people who invent technology. Look at these examples. Compare the original meaning with the new meaning. How are the words related?

Word	Original meanings	New meaning
Internet	*inter*—a prefix that means to connect different places. *network*—a system of connected roads or communication systems.	*Internet*—a large computer network used by people and organizations around the world.
browser	A person who looks over things in a slow, delayed way; a shopper who looks at products but does not buy them.	A computer tool that helps people find information on the Internet.
surf	To ride on ocean waves as they break on ocean shore; to change the channels on a TV, looking for the best programs.	To search from place to place on the Internet.
site (website)	An area or place.	An Internet address; a place on the Internet.

▭ Reading for a Purpose

EXERCISE 3   **Using headings**

Before you read Selection 1, look at the headings. Notice that all the selection headings are questions. As you read, underline or highlight keywords in the paragraph that answer these questions. Paragraph 2 has been done for you as an example. The question that introduces paragraph 2 is "Whose website is it?" According to the paragraph, you will visit different types of websites, including government (.gov), education (.edu), commercial (.com), and organization (.org).

Reading Selection 1

THINKING CRITICALLY ABOUT THE INTERNET

1   Don't expect to find these warnings on the Internet. No one has checked out the ideas you find there for truthfulness. No logic police[1] watch the Internet looking for violators. It is up to you to avoid being a victim. Here are the most important questions to ask when you use the Internet.

What Type of Site Is This?

2   You will visit many different sites. Websites have different types including government (.gov), education (.edu), commercial (.com), and organization (.org). Each site will reflect the bias[2] of the people who created and maintain it. Knowing whose site it is will help you evaluate how accurate the information you find there is. When looking at a website, you should notice what type of site it is.

1. **log•ic po•lice** (lŏj´ĭk pə-lēs´) *n.* Persons who would control or keep in logical order.
2. **bi•as** (bī´əs) *n.* A prejudice.

What Function Does the Site Serve?

3   Every site has a specific purpose. Generally speaking, government and education sites are designed to provide the public with important or helpful information. On the other hand, commercial sites are designed to sell products and/or services.

4   Expect the companies that have commercial websites to say good things about their own products and services and to ignore faults and defects. Don't be surprised if they imply that their competitors' products and services are inferior. Be aware that such statements may or may not be true and should be tested rather than assumed to be true.

Which Statements Are Fact and Which Are Opinions?

5   A fact is generally accepted reality, something that informed people agree about. An opinion, on the other hand, is a belief or a conclusion that not everyone agrees about. It is important not to confuse opinion with fact.

6   It is more difficult to tell fact from opinion on the Internet than on TV or in magazines. This is because anyone can express his or her ideas on the Internet.

Where Can Statements of Fact be Confirmed?[3]

7   Statements that are offered as fact may in reality be false. (Even honest people make mistakes, and not everyone is honest.) Suppose you encounter the statement: "The divorce rate has tripled in the past 20 years." This is written like a statement of fact. But is it factual? In other words, is it accurate? You should probably check this fact to make sure. You can check other Internet sites, books or magazines to see if they agree with this statistic.

Does the Evidence Support the Opinion?

8   In making this decision, consider all the evidence you have found. That includes the kind of evidence that supports the opinion. Remember, that your own personal observation and experience count as evidence.

Source: Adapted from Ruggiero, V. R. (1999). *Becoming a Critical Thinker*. Boston: Houghton Mifflin, pp. 111–112.

---

3. **con•firmed** (kən-fûrmd´) *adj.* Firmly established; proven.

▭ Assessing Your Learning: Thinking Critically about the Internet

Demonstrating Comprehension

EXERCISE 4 Identifying main ideas

The main idea of a paragraph is the principal point the author wants you to understand. It is the biggest idea in the paragraph, and it is different from a detail. A detail is a specific fact that supports the main idea. *Review each paragraph. Circle the letter next to the sentence that best expresses the main idea. The first one has been done for you as an example.*

1. Paragraph 1
   - a. You must check the Internet for truthfulness. (*main idea*)
   - b. No logic police watch the Internet. (*detail*)
   - c. Questions are important on the Internet. (*This is not true. The paragraph says questions about the Internet are important.*)
   - d. Avoid the Internet. (*This is not true. The paragraph says to avoid being a victim.*)

2. Paragraph 2
   - a. You will visit different sites.
   - b. You should ask who created the site so that you can evaluate it.
   - c. Government = .gov; education = .edu; commercial = .com; organization = .org.
   - d. The best kind of site is a .com.

3. Paragraphs 3 and 4
   - a. Governmental and educational sites provide information, while commercial sites sell products.
   - b. All sites serve different functions.
   - c. Commercial sites may or may not have factual information.
   - d. Competitors' products and services are inferior.

4. Paragraphs 5 and 6
   - a. Facts and opinions are easy to confuse.
   - b. TV and magazines are more truthful than the Internet.
   - c. You should assume that most things on the Internet are opinion.
   - d. Anyone can express ideas on the Internet.

5. Paragraphs 7 and 8
   - a. The divorce rate has tripled.
   - b. You should check facts on the Internet in books and magazines.
   - c. It is difficult to confirm statements from Internet sites.
   - d. Even honest people make mistakes, and not everyone is honest.

▭ Learning Vocabulary

EXERCISE 5 **Practicing dictionary skills**

Look at this dictionary definition for the word bias. *Then respond to the following items.*

> **bias** (bī´əs) *noun* **1.** A general tendency: *She has a bias against wasting money.* **2.** Prejudice: *He has a bias against people who wear glasses.*

1. Find the word *bias* in paragraph 2. Which definition of the word fits the way it is used in this reading selection? _____

   _____

2. Notice that, in both examples, *bias* is followed by the word *against.* What do you have a bias against? Write three sentences using the word *bias.*

   a. _I have a bias against. . ._____

   b. _____

   c. _____

EXERCISE 6 **Studying academic vocabulary**

These words from Reading Selection 1 are commonly found in academic texts. Study the list of words below, and then learn them by following these guidelines.

1. Number a paper from 1 to 17. Copy these words, leaving space for a definition. Notice that the paragraph location is provided in parentheses next to the word.
2. Write a definition, synonym, or translation for the words you already know.
3. Compare your list with a partner's. Help each other learn new words.
4. Share your list with your classmates. Your instructor can help you define the words you do not know.

1. logic (¶1)	**7.** function (¶3)	**13.** assume (¶4)
2. site (¶2)	**8.** specific (¶3)	**14.** conclusion (¶5)
3. bias (¶2)	**9.** design (¶3)	**15.** encounter (¶7)
4. maintain (¶2)	**10.** ignore (¶4)	**16.** statistic (¶7)
5. evaluate (¶2)	**11.** aware (¶4)	**17.** evidence (¶8)
6. accurate (¶2)	**12.** imply (¶4)	

EXERCISE 7   **Practicing academic words**

Practice using the academic words by completing this crossword puzzle.

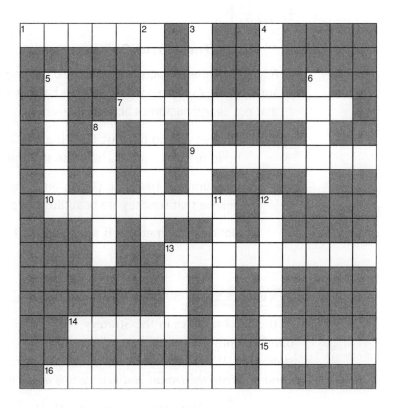

Across

1. Do not pay attention to
7. Result
9. Purpose; task; job
10. Facts or data used for proof
13. Number, exact amount
14. Conscious; sensitive
15. Don't say directly
16. Correct, exact

Down

2. Meet; see
3. Not general
4. Belief or prejudice for or against something
5. Suppose, believe
6. Reason
8. Plan, purpose
11. Check to see if something is accurate
12. Keep the same; uphold; preserve
13. Place, location

▭ Questions for Review

S T R A T E G Y

Fact versus Opinion

A fact is a generally accepted reality, something that informed people agree about. An opinion, on the other hand, is a belief or conclusion that not everyone agrees about. For example:

> The sun rises in the east. (This is a fact. The sun always comes up in the east, moves across the sky, and sets in the west.)

> The sunrise is beautiful. (This is an opinion. Some people may believe that sunrises are beautiful, but others may disagree.)

> Noticing if something is an opinion or fact is important.

EXERCISE **8** **Working with fact and opinion**

In the two examples in the Strategy box, it is easy to tell fact from opinion. Sometimes it is more difficult. *Read each of the following statements. Write F if the statement is a fact. Write O if the statement is an opinion. Write the reason you believe it is a fact or an opinion.*

1. ___O___ Here are the most important questions to ask when you use the Internet.

   Reason: ___"Important" shows opinion._____

2. _____ Websites are of different types, including government (.gov), education (.edu), commercial (.com), and organization (.org).

   Reason: _____

3. _____ Expect the companies that have commercial websites to say good things about their own products and services and to ignore faults and defects.

   Reason: _____

4. _____ A fact is generally accepted reality, something that informed people agree about.

Reason: _____

5. _____ An opinion is a belief or a conclusion that not everyone agrees about.

Reason: _____

6. _____ It is probably best to assume that most things printed on the Internet are opinion unless you are certain they are true.

Reason: _____

▭ Focusing on Technology

EXERCISE 9   Evaluating websites

This chart has the questions from Reading Selection 1. Your instructor will provide you with 2 websites, a .com and a .gov, for you to compare. Practice what you learned about the Internet by answering the questions about each website.

	Website 1	Website 2
Whose site is it?		
What is the function of the site?		
What are statements of fact?		
What are statements of opinion?		
Where could you confirm the information?		

⬜ Questions for Review and Discussion

EXERCISE 10   Participating in a group mini-presentation

Work with a group of three or four other students. Find two websites about the same topic. Make a chart similar to the one you used for the previous exercise. Make a presentation to your classmates explaining why your group thinks these websites are truthful or not.

Here are some possible topics you could search on the Internet:

- Websites about your city or community
- Websites about a place you would like to visit
- Websites about a musician, athlete, or author
- Websites about a historical event

⬜ Linking Concepts

EXERCISE 11   Writing in your reading journal

Answer the following questions in your journal:

1. Write about what you learned from doing the group project.
2. Reading Selection 1 tells you to use your experiences to confirm the truthfulness of websites. Explain what experiences you have had that you could use to confirm the truthfulness of a website.
3. What do you think is more helpful for doing research—books and magazines or the Internet? Explain.

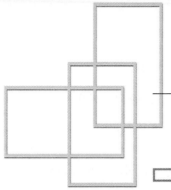

Reading Assignment 2

▭ Getting Ready to Read

EXERCISE 12 Participating in class discussion

Discuss these questions, and complete the tasks with your classmates:

1. Brainstorm a list of different types of technology that people use every day. Which of these were not used ten years ago?

Common technology now	Common ten years ago?
1. Cell phones	no

2. Look at the boxes called "Main Idea" and "Why It Matters" from the beginning of Reading Selection 2. What do you think this reading selection will be about?

Main Idea	Why It Matters
New technology is growing quickly. It can change the world in positive ways. However, it also creates challenges for people around the world.	Technology has already changed communications and medicine. In the future it may help solve other problems.

EXERCISE 13   **Previewing vocabulary**

With your classmates, make a list of different kinds of jobs people have.

In North America, jobs have often been divided into two types:
white-collar jobs and **blue-collar jobs.**

- **White-collar workers** are professionals who usually work in an office.
- **Blue-collar workers** work with their hands. They usually make, repair, or clean something.

Use the list of jobs you made with your classmates. Write the jobs under one of the following categories.

Blue-Collar Jobs   **White-Collar Jobs**   **Other**

_____   _____   _____

_____   _____   _____

_____   _____   _____

Why do you think professional jobs are called white-collar and manual jobs are called blue-collar?

Master Student Tip

Reading selections have particular organizational patterns. The paragraphs in Selection 2 follow a very common pattern. A general statement comes first, and then it is supported with examples.

🔲 Reading for a Purpose

This first paragraph is an example of general statement + examples pattern:

People have always used science to find new ways to do things. But technological change has increased very quickly in the last 50 years. For instance, the development of the silicon chip has brought revolutions in electronics and computers. In addition, research in biology has produced great advances in medicine. Biologists can even clone living creatures.

The terms *For instance* and *In addition* tell us that the sentences that follow are examples to support the sentences before it.

EXERCISE 14 Noticing words that signal examples

As you read the text, circle the words that signal examples and write a list of these words.

Reading Selection 2

TECHNOLOGY CHANGES PEOPLE'S LIVES

Main Idea	Why It Matters
New technology is growing quickly. It can change the world in positive ways. However, it also creates challenges for people around the world.	Technology has already changed communications and medicine. In the future it may help solve other problems.

1   People have always used science to find new ways to do things. But technological change has increased very quickly in the last 50 years. For instance, the development of the silicon chip[1] has brought revolutions[2] in electronics and computers. In addition, research in biology has produced great advances in medicine. Biologists can even clone[3] living creatures.

A Revolution in Electronics

2   New forms of electronic circuits[4] have made computers possible. Computers and advances in communications change the way people use information. For one thing, they increase the speed at which information can be transported.

The Influence of Computers

3   The earliest and most basic use of computers was for computing. That is, doing things like figuring out math problems. Today we use a calculator to figure out problems that were done on computers in the past. Electronic circuits have become faster. Computers are able to solve problems more quickly. Powerful computers can make billions of computations every second.

1. **sil•i•con chip** (sĭl-ĭ-kŏn′ chĭp) *n.* An electronic material used in building computers.
2. **rev•o•lu•tion** (rĕv′ə-lōō′shən) *n.* Sudden and important changes.
3. **clone** (klōn) *n.* Produce a copy of somebody or something; reproduced asexually.
4. **e•lec•tro•nic cir•cuit** (ĭ-lĕk-trŏn′ĭk sûr′kĭt) *n.* System of electrically connected parts.

4   The ability to compute quickly makes computers very helpful. For example, they are used to guide rockets and satellites into space. Air traffic controllers[5] use them to check airline traffic. Many cars use computers. Also, banks use computers to keep track of accounts.

Information Spreads in New Ways

5   Electronic technology has also had a great impact on how people communicate. People use cellular phones, fax machines, and computers to move information. As a result, people can do business, or just chat[6] from great distances. These technologies have made the world closer.

6   The Internet is one of the most exciting ways for people to communicate. People can use the Internet to find information. Businesses advertise their goods on the Internet. Governments use the Internet to provide information. In addition, people around the world can use chat rooms[7] and electronic mail (or e-mail)[8] to send messages to one another. The result has been an amazing growth in the use of the Internet. In 1993, there were only 50 Internet sites. By 1998, there were too many sites to accurately count. Internet traffic was doubling every 100 days.

How Technology Transforms the World Economy

7   Electronic technology has led to changes in the world economy. For instance, computer robots now help to make many products, such as cars. Modern communications allow banking to be done electronically. Technological changes have both positive and negative effects on businesses and workers.

The Workplace Changes

8   Rapid communications and information transmission have helped to transform workplaces around the world. Many white-collar workers now "telecommute."[9] They do their jobs by computer from home. Business people can do business around the world,

---

5. **air traf•fic con•trol•ler** (âr trăf´ĭk kən-trō´ler) *n.* Persons who control or regulate the landing and takeoff of airplanes.
6. **chat** (chăt) *v.* To communicate electronically with written messages that are exchanged instantly.
7. **chat room** (chăt rōōm) *n.* Internet site where several people can chat at the same time.
8. **e-mail** (ē´māl´) *n.* A system for sending messages through computers.
9. **tel•e•com•mute** (tĕl´ĭ-kə-mōōt) *v.* To work at home using a computer connected to the network of one's employer.

from almost anywhere. They use telephones, fax machines, and computers to do their work. The Internet can instantly give workers the information they need. Nowadays some professionals do not have to go to their offices.

9   Technology affects manufacturing. Robots perform jobs that were once done by people. For this reason, many companies have cut the number of workers. Employment is shifting from blue-collar industries to high-tech industries. Many workers are forced to improve their skills to keep their jobs. This is because high-tech industries[10] need workers with more technical skills.

Economic Domination[11]

10   High-tech workplaces are found mainly in industrialized countries.[12] Industrialized countries include the United States, Japan, and the countries of Western Europe. This causes a problem for less-developed countries.[13] The industrialized nations dominate less-developed countries because they have technology. Technology helps make the developed countries[14] economically stronger. This economic strength gives the developed countries control over economic aid[15] in less-developed countries. Technology also gives the developed nations better military equipment. They can use this equipment to control the governments of less-developed countries.

Source: Ruggiero, V. (1999). *Becoming a Critical Thinker*. Boston: Houghton Mifflin, pp. 111–112.

10. **high-tech in•dus•try** (hī′tĕk′ ĭn′də-strē) *n*. Business requiring computers and advanced
11. **dom•i•na•tion** (dŏm′ə-nā′shən) *n*. Control or power over something.
12. **in•dus•tri•a•li•zed coun•try** (ĭn-dŭs′trē-ə-līzd kŭn′trē) *n*. Country having highly developed industries.
13. **less-de•ve•loped coun•try** (lĕs dĭ-vĕl′əpd kŭn′trē) *n*.Country having a low level of economic development in technology in comparison to other countries.
14. **de•ve•loped coun•try** (dĭ-vĕl′əpd kŭn′trē) *n*. Country having many industries and better living conditions.
15. **e•con•o•mic aid** (ĕk′ə-nŏm′ĭk ād) *n*. Help or assistance in the form of money.

 **Assessing Your Learning: Technology Changes People's Lives**

Demonstrating Comprehension

> **STRATEGY**
>
> **The Main Idea**
>
> When trying to find the main idea, ask yourself, What does the author want me to know about this topic? The main idea is composed of two parts: the topic and the controlling idea. The topic, as you have already learned, is what the passage is about. The controlling idea is what the author wants you to know about the topic. The main idea is a complete sentence. It is the most general idea in the paragraph.

Look at the following sentence:

There are <u>different types</u> of <u>websites</u>.

1. What is this sentence about?   Websites.
2. What does it say about websites?   There are different types.

As you continue to read a passage, you will see the details that support the main idea. In other words, the other sentences in the passage provide information about the main idea. When choosing a main idea, if you are uncertain of your choice, reread the passage and make sure the choice you made is what the rest of the passage is about.

Think about how the following details support the main idea, "There are different types of websites."

a. Websites have different types of sites.
b. Each site will reflect the bias of the people who created and maintain it.
c. Knowing whose site it is will help you evaluate how accurate the information you find there is.

EXERCISE 15   Finding the main idea

The statements below are the main ideas of each of the paragraphs of Reading Selection 2. They are not in the same order as in the reading selection. Match each main idea with its paragraph number. One example has been done for you.

1. _____ Technology has changed white-collar jobs.

2. _____ There have been rapid changes in electronics.

3. _____ Technology keeps powerful countries strong.

4. ___1___ Technology is changing rapidly.

5. _____ Technology changes how people communicate.

6. _____ Technology affects the world economy.

7. _____ Computers are found in lots of different places.

8. _____ Technology has changed blue-collar jobs.

9. _____ The Internet is changing people's lives.

10. _____ Computers were originally used like calculators.

▭ Learning Vocabulary

POWER GRAMMAR

Word Roots

Some words have the same roots but are used in different forms. For example, here are three different forms of the word *computer*:

Sentence	Meaning
We had to **compute** the answer to the math problem.	*Make a calculation; do arithmetic*
When we finished, we compared our **computations**.	*Arithmetic problems*
A **computer** makes it easier to solve difficult problems.	*A machine that makes calculations, solves problems, and stores information.*

EXERCISE 16   **Working with word families**

The following chart shows some other words from Reading Selection 2 that have the same roots in different forms.

- *Find the words in the reading selection.*
- *Write the number of the paragraph you find them in.*
- *Notice how the words are related.*
- *Write a definition for each bold word as in the example in the Power Grammar box. If you do not know the definition, find the definition in a dictionary.*

Sentence	Paragraph number	Definition
Advances in electronics have revolutionized modern society.	¶ 2	Electronics is the study of electricity and how it works.
Electronic circuits move electricity.		
Economic problems are often found in developing countries.		
The **economy** of developed countries is based on industry.		
Computer programmers provide **technical** support.		
Technological advances have changed our lives in the last fifty years.		

Sentence	Paragraph number	Definition
Technology has positive and negative effects.		
Technology helped **transform** the modern world.		
The **transition** from one lifestyle to another can be difficult.		
Computers make it easy to **transport** information.		
We received an electronic **transmission**.		
Developed countries **dominate** less developed countries.		
Domination is based on power.		

EXERCISE 17   **Expanding word families**

Use a dictionary to find other words that have the same roots. Write a definition for each of these words. The first one has been done for you as an example.

Root	New word	Definition
1. *compute-*	Computerize	To put information into a computer.
2. *electro-*		
3. *econom-*		
4. *tech-*		
5. *trans-*		
6. *domini-*		

EXERCISE 18   **Studying academic vocabulary**

These words from Reading Selection 2 are commonly found in academic texts. Study the list of words below, and then learn them by following these guidelines:

1. Number a paper from 1 to 23. Copy these words, leaving space for a definition. The paragraph location is provided in parentheses next to the word.
2. Write a definition, synonym, or translation for the words you already know.
3. Compare your list with a partner's. Help each other learn new words.
4. Share your list with your classmates. Your instructor can help you define the words you do not know.

1. challenges (¶1)
2. technological (¶1)
3. research (¶1)
4. revolution (¶1)
5. computer (¶2)
6. compute (¶3)
7. computations (¶3)
8. traffic (¶4)
9. impact (¶5)
10. communicate (¶5)
11. sites (¶6)
12. accurately (¶6)
13. transform (¶7)
14. positive (¶7)
15. negative (¶7)
16. jobs (¶8)
17. professionals (¶8)
18. shifting (¶9)
19. technical (¶9)
20. economic (¶10)
21. aid (¶10)
22. military (¶10)
23. equipment (¶10)

Questions for Review

EXERCISE **19** **Reading critically**

List some examples of how industrialized or developed countries use technology to dominate less-developed countries.

1. _____
   _____

2. _____
   _____

3. _____
   _____

4. _____
   _____

Master Student Tip

Relating What You Know to a Reading Text

Reading critically means you think about what you are reading. Is what the author says true? What information do you already know that supports what the author is saying?

Paragraph 10 of Reading Selection 2 says: "The industrialized nations dominate less-developed countries because they have technology." In your experience, is this statement true or not?

⌨ Questions for Review and Discussion

EXERCISE 20 Analyzing pros and cons in a small group

Work with a group of three or four other students. Do the following activities:

1. *Make a list of reasons why computers can be positive or negative.*

Computers are positive because . . .	Computers are negative because . . .
_____	_____
_____	_____
_____	_____
_____	_____
_____	_____
_____	_____

2. *Reading Selection 2 says computers are used in cars and banks and by air traffic controllers. What are some other uses of computers? Make a list with your group.*

a. People who need computers to work. . .

bank tellers _____

air traffic controllers _____

_____

_____

b. We find computerized equipment in. . .

cars _____

_____

_____

_____

▭ Linking Concepts

EXERCISE 21   Writing in your reading journal

Answer the following questions in your journal:

1. Describe the positive and negative effects of computers. Use the chart your group made to help you.
2. Do you agree or disagree with the following statement? "The world is smaller because of computers." Explain why.
3. Describe how computers affect your life today.
4. Describe how computers and technology will change our lives in the future.

EXERCISE 22   Practicing with main ideas and support

Think about how each numbered sentence in the example paragraph below expresses or supports a main idea. Read the sample chart, and then complete the blank charts in a similar manner.

Example 1

1 Advanced technology is able to provide us with diverse possibilities to enhance security and make communication faster. 2 As a result of technology, advanced weapons have been created to establish security and power in global competition. 3 Technology has also intensified our means of communication, not only through television and radio but also with faxes, e-mail, cellular phones, and the Internet, which are all means of instantaneous individual communication that have become common in the past decade. 4 These advances in technology have great influence worldwide, and they continue to change societies.

Source: Adapted from Perry, M., Chase, M., Jacob, J.R.., Jacob, M.C. & Von Laue, T.H. (2000). *Western Civilization Ideas, Politics & Society.* Boston: Houghton Mifflin Company, pp. 904–905.

Study this explanation chart.

What is this passage about?	advanced technology
What is it telling you about advanced technology?	It has enhanced security and made communication faster.
Sentence 1	is the main idea.
Sentence 2	tells you about the weapons created for our security.
Sentence 3	mentions different modes of speedy communication we now have.
Sentence 4	makes a second general statement about advanced technology.

A main idea can be found in the beginning, middle, or end of a passage. Sometimes the author begins the paragraph with the main idea, as in the previous example. Other times, the author may provide some type of introduction or background information before the main idea. In this case, the main idea will not be the first sentence. Or, an author may start by providing specific details that lead up to the main idea. As a result, the main idea will be found at the end of the paragraph.

Example 2

1 Science and technology, more closely related than ever, have increased human control over nature beyond the imagination of earlier ages. 2 Physicists have explored the atom down to the smallest components of matter. 3 Biologists have uncovered the genetic structures of living matter. 4 Human beings have set foot on the moon.

Source: Perry, M., Chase, M., Jacob, J.R., Jacob, M.C., & Von Laue, T.H. (2000). *Western Civilization Ideas, Politics & Society* (6th ed.). Boston: Houghton Mifflin Company, p. 902.

Complete this explanation chart.

What is this passage about?	
What is it telling you about _____?	
Sentence 1	*is the main idea.*
Sentence 2	
Sentence 3	
Sentence 4	

Example 3

1 Who would not want to drive a powerful car? 2 Well, technology also shapes the style of individual transportation. 3 There are cars that work on batteries to reduce the pollution produced by the exhaust fumes, which are polluting cities. 4 So for those who are concerned about the environment, one of these cars might be quite suitable. 5 Other cars are built smaller in order to save gas. 6 With petroleum prices getting higher, some people prefer to drive a car that will not consume too much gas. 7 And then, there are those who prefer the comfort of a spacious car no matter how much gas it consumes. 8 Of course, the powerful cars driven by the very powerful can be small, but they still consume a lot of gas. 9 They are stylish and expensive to buy and to maintain. 10 Pick your style!

Source: Adapted from Perry, M., Chase, M., Jacob, J.R., Jacob, M.C., & Von Laue, T.H. (2000). *Western Civilization Ideas, Politics & Society* (6th ed.). Boston: Houghton Mifflin Company, p. 902. Remaining sentences written by author.

Complete this explanation chart.

What is this passage about?	
What is it telling you about _____?	
Sentence 1	
Sentence 2	*is the main idea.*
Sentence 3	
Sentence 4	
Sentence 5	
Sentence 6	
Sentence 7	
Sentence 8	
Sentence 9	
Sentence 10	

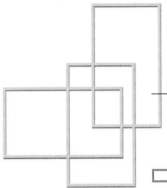

Reading Assignment 3

☐ Getting Ready to Read

EXERCISE 23 Participating in class discussion

Discuss the following questions with your classmates:

1. What is e-mail?
2. What is a chat room?
3. What is a newsgroup?
4. What is the difference between e-mail, a chat room, and a newsgroup?
5. Have you ever sent an e-mail?
6. Have you ever participated in a chat room?
7. What kinds of things do people write in each?

EXERCISE 24 Previewing vocabulary

Use a dictionary to help answer the following questions:

1. a: What does *etiquette* mean?
   b: What do you think the word *netiquette* means?

2. a: What does *emotion* mean?
   b: What does *icon* mean?
   c: What do you think the word *emoticon* means?

3. a: What are flames?
   b: What do you think the word *flaming* means?

▭ Reading for a Purpose

EXERCISE 25   Listing "shoulds" and "should nots"

Reading Selection 3 explains proper ways to act when you communicate with someone through the Internet. As you read this selection, make a list of things you should do and things you should not do when communicating through the Internet. After you read, share your list with a partner. Did you write the same things?

Do's	Don'ts
_____	_____
_____	_____
_____	_____
_____	_____
_____	_____
_____	_____
_____	_____
_____	_____
_____	_____
_____	_____
_____	_____

Reading Selection 3

PRACTICE "NETIQUETTE": BE KIND WHILE YOU'RE ONLINE

1   Most people wouldn't walk into a meeting and dominate the conversation. They do not cut people off[1] in the middle of sentences. Yet even well-meaning people can do the online equivalent of these things. These people could use a lesson in "netiquette."

2   Netiquette is a collection of informal rules that apply to people who "talk" to each other though personal computers. Think of these rules as etiquette[2] for the Internet. Through e-mail, newsgroups, and chat rooms, the Internet puts you in touch with a worldwide community. Etiquette is important in any community—online[3] or in person. You're more likely to be accepted in a community when you know the unspoken rules and remember how people like to be treated.

---

1. **cut peo•ple off** *tr. v.* To stop or shut off a person who is talking.
2. **et•i•quette** (ĕt´ĭ-kĕt´) *n.* The forms and rules of proper behavior required by custom among people.
3. **on•line** (ŏn´līn´) *adj.* Connected to or controlled by a computer.

Put Out the Flames

3   One thing you should avoid when communicating online is flaming. Flaming takes place when someone sends a hostile[4] online message. To create positive relationships when you're online, avoid sending such messages.

4   Some Internet users believe occasional "flaming" is all right. These users argue that anger is appropriate when people are face to face. Then, it should also be appropriate online. But few advocate "flame wars"—a long series of insults[5] exchanged between a few people. This kind of exchange can dominate a newsgroup[6] or chatroom.[7]

5   Many newsgroups have written policies about what kinds of messages are permitted. Often you'll receive e-mail with these rules when you subscribe.[8] When you're new to a newsgroup, spend a little time reading messages without replying to them. By observing what people write, you'll learn the unwritten rules for that group.

4. **hos•tile** (hŏs′təl) *adj.* Relating to or characteristics of an enemy.
5. **insult** (ĭn-sŭlt′) *n.* Offensive action or remarks.
6. **news•group** (nōōz′grōōp′) *n.* An area on a computer network, especially the Internet, devoted to the discussion of a specific topic.
7. **chat•room** (chăt′ rōōm′) *n.* A website where people can have online conversations with others who are on the Internet.
8. **sub•scribe** (səb-scrīb′) *intr.v.* To pay regularly for something such as issues of a magazine or tickets to a series of performances; to have regular messages about events sent through the Internet.

Respect Others' Time and Privacy

6 People often use the Internet hoping to save time—not waste it. You can help them by typing brief messages. Get into the habit of getting to the point. If you create your own webpage, limit its download time[9] by using simple graphics. Complex graphics take a long time to download; this can make people frustrated. Update[10] your page regularly and include your e-mail address. Finally, let other people open their own e-mail messages. Reading people's e-mail is the same as opening letters from their mailboxes.

Keep the Medium in Mind

7 When you are communicating by computer, there is no nonverbal[11] communication. This means there are no hand gestures[12] and facial expressions.[13] In face-to-face conversation, you use the subtle cues[14] of nonverbal communication to help you understand another person's message. But when your link to another person takes place only through words on a screen, those cues vanish.

9. **down• load time** (doun′lōd′ tīm) *n.* Length of time it takes to transfer information from a central computer to another computer.
10. **up•date** (ŭp dāt′) *tv.v.* To bring up to date; inform of new information or recent changes.
11. **non•ver•bal** (nŏn-vûr′bəl) *adj.* Not using words.
12. **hand ges•ture** (hănd jĕs′chər) *n.* Movement of the hands.
13. **fa•cial ex•pres•sion** (fā′shəl ĭk-sprĕsh′ən) *n.* Movements of the face to communicate.
14. **cue** (kyo͞o) *n.* Word or signal for action.

8   Use humor—especially sarcasm[15]—with caution. A joke that's funny when you tell it to a person might offend someone when you write it and send it by computer. Especially, use emoticons with care. Emoticons are combinations of keyboard characters that represent an emotion, such as :>). (Turn the book sideways to see a smiling face at the end of the previous sentence.) Emoticons are informal. They may not be appropriate for some Internet-based communications. For example, you would not want to send e-mails with emoticons to someone who might hire you for a job.

9   Netiquette also means avoiding messages THAT APPEAR IN ALL UPPERCASE LETTERS. Writing with the shift key[16] held down to make capitals is equal to shouting during a face-to-face conversation.

Remember—Behind Every Computer Is a Person

10   The heart of netiquette is to remember that the person on the other end is a human being. Virginia Shea, author of *Netiquette*, suggests that you remember the prime rule of netiquette by asking yourself one question whenever you're at the keyboard:[17] Would you say it to the person's face?

Source: Adapted from Ellis, D. (2000). *Becoming a Master Student*. Boston: Houghton Mifflin, p. 298.

15. **sar•casm** (sär′kăz′əm) *n.* A sharply mocking, often ironic remark intended to wound.
16. **shift key** (shĭft kē) *n.* Key on a computer keyboard that changes letters to UPPERCASE.
17. **key•board** (kē′bôrd′) *n.* A set of keys, as on a piano or a computer.

⬛ **Demonstrating Comprehension**

EXERCISE 26 **Identifying main ideas**

Review Reading Selection 3 again. What is the main idea of each section?
Read the sentences and circle the one that best expresses the main idea.
Compare your main idea with your partner's. The first one has been done
for you as an example.

Section	Main idea
Practice "Netiquette"	(a) It is important to use "netiquette," or good manners while you are communicating online. b) People who dominate the Net do this.
Put Out the Flames	a) Flaming creates positive relationships online. b) Sending someone a hostile message online is called flaming.
Respect Others' Time and Privacy	a) Reading people's e-mail is the same as opening letters from their mailboxes. b) Respecting people's time and privacy is important.
Keep the Medium in Mind	a) When you communicate online, avoid messages that may offend or be misunderstood. b) Use humor with caution.
Remember—Behind Every Computer Is a Person	a) There is a person on the other end. b) You should question yourself when you're at the keyboard.

▢ Learning Vocabulary

EXERCISE 27 **Studying prefixes that make opposites**

Look at these four words from Reading Selection 3. Go back to the reading selection and underline these words. What do they have in common?

1. informal (¶ 2) **3.** unwritten (¶ 5)
2. unspoken (¶ 2) **4.** nonverbal (¶ 7)

STRATEGY

Prefixes

In each word, the prefix (*in-*, *un-*, and *non-*) makes the word an opposite. *Informal* means "not formal." *Unspoken* means "not spoken." *Unwritten* means "not written," and *nonverbal* means "not verbal."

Here are other words with prefixes that mean "not."

Impossible means "not possible."

Disinterested means "not interested."

EXERCISE 28 **Working with prefixes**

Do you know other words that change their meanings because of these prefixes? Work with a partner. In the chart below, list as many words as you can think of that have an opposite meaning when these prefixes are added. Examples are provided.

in-	un-	non-	im-	dis-
informal	unspoken	nonverbal	impossible	disinterested

EXERCISE 29 Studying academic vocabulary

These words from Reading Selection 3 are commonly found in academic texts. If you do not know the meaning of a word, you can look it up in a dictionary. However, often in English a word has more than one meaning. Reread the sentences each of these vocabulary words is in. Look at the dictionary definitions of the words. Choose the definition that goes with how the word is used in the text.

1. dominate (¶ 1)
2. equivalent (¶ 1)
3. community (¶ 2)
4. create (¶ 3)
5. positive (¶ 3)
6. appropriate (¶ 4)
7. advocate (¶ 4)
8. series (¶ 4)
9. policies (¶ 5)

10. finally (¶ 6)
11. medium (¶ 7)
12. communication (¶ 7)
13. subtle (¶ 7)
14. link (¶ 7)
15. equal (¶ 9)
16. prime (¶ 10)
17. author (¶ 10)

Choose the definition that goes with how the word was used in the reading selection.

▭ Definitions

1. **advocate** *noun, verb* (¶ 4)
   1. A person who supports a cause.
   2. Push for something.
   3. A lawyer.

2. **appropriate** *verb, adjective* (¶ 4)
   1. To make money available.
   2. Suitable or correct.
   3. Take without permission or take with force.

3. **author** *noun, verb* (¶ 10)
   1. A person who writes books.
   2. To be the writer of something.
   3. Someone who causes something.

4. **communication** *noun* (¶ 7)
   1. The act of passing on information.
   2. A message.
   3. Understanding the message.

5. **community** *noun, adjective* (¶ 2)
    1. A group of people.
    2. A group of people with the same racial and religious background.
    3. Belonging to and maintained by and for the local community.

6. **create** *verb* (¶ 3)
    1. To give life to.
    2. Bring into existence.
    3. Pursue a creative activity; be engaged in a creative activity.

7. **dominate** *verb* (¶ 1)
    1. To have more.
    2. Be in control.
    3. Look down on.

8. **equal** *noun, verb, adjective* (¶ 9)
    1. A person who is at the same social level as another.
    2. The same as.
    3. Alike.

9. **equivalent** *noun, adjective* (¶ 1)
    1. A person or thing equal to another in value.
    2. Equal in amount or value.
    3. Being essentially equal to something. *"a wish that was equivalent to a command"*

10. **finally** *adverb* (¶ 6)
    1. After a long period of time.
    2. The item at the end.
    3. As the end result.

11. **link** *noun, verb* (¶ 7)
    1. To connect things.
    2. Make a logical or causal connection.
    3. Be joined.

12. **medium** *noun, adjective* (¶ 7)
    1. A means to communicate.
    2. In the middle; not big or small.
    3. Someone who speaks with spirits.

13. **positive** *adjective* (¶ 3)
    1. Hopeful; optimistic.
    2. Certain; definite.
    3. Affirmative.

14. **prime** *noun, adjective* (¶ 10)
    1. A number that has no factor but itself and 1.
    2. First in rank or degree.
    3. The superior type.

▭ Questions for Review

EXERCISE 30 **Talking about what you have read**

One way to remember what you read is to discuss it with someone else. Try to remember what you read in Selection 3.

1. *On the lines below, write as many details as you can remember from each section. Do not look at the reading again.*
2. *Compare your answers with a partner's.*
3. *Add any details you may have missed.*
4. *Reread the selection and check your answers.*

▭ Practice "Netiquette": Be Kind While You're Online

Introduction

_____

Put Out the Flames

_____

Respect Others' Time and Privacy

_____

Keep the Medium in Mind

_____

Remember—Behind Every Computer Is a Person

_____

⬜ Focusing on Technology

EXERCISE 31   **Understanding emoticons**

*Here are some examples of emoticons. Discuss them with a partner: When would you use these emoticons? Whom would you use them with? Whom would you **never** use them with? What keyboard keys were used to make these emoticons?*

Happy, smiling, laughing

> :-) smiling; agreeing
>
> :-D laughing
>
> |-) hee hee
>
> :-> hey hey
>
> ;-) so happy, I'm crying
>
> \~/ full glass; my glass is full

Teasing, mischievous

> ;-) winking; just kidding
>
> '-) winking; just kidding
>
> :*) clowning

Affirming, supporting

> :-o "Wow!"
>
> ^5 high five
>
> ^   thumbs up

Unhappy, sad

> :-(frowning
>
> :(sad
>
> :-[pouting
>
> _/ "my glass is empty"

Angry, sarcastic

>:-< angry

:-@ screaming

:-V shouting

Trying to communicate

:-& tongue-tied

:-S incoherent

:( ) can't stop talking

Feeling stupid or tired

:~/ mixed up

l-O yawning

l-I asleep

:-6 exhausted; wiped out

Surprised

:> What?

:Q What?

:-o "uhh oh!" OR surprise

:O shocked

8-l eyes wide with surprise

Hugs and kisses

: * kisses

:-X a big wet kiss!

:-{} blowing a kiss

[ ] hugs

(( )):** hugs and kisses

((((name)))) hug

Miscellaneous

:-* Oops!

O :-) being an angel (at heart, at least)

⬜ Questions for Review and Discussion

EXERCISE 32 **Experimenting on the Internet**

Work with a partner. Do the following activities:

1. With your partner, write an e-mail that breaks one of the rules of netiquette. Do not send the e-mail. Instead, print it out and give it to another set of partners in your class. See if they can find the rule you broke. Discuss how a person might feel if he or she received that e-mail.
2. Work with a partner. Invent your own emoticon. Explain to your classmates what your emoticon means.
3. Enroll yourself in a chat group. Do the members of your chat group follow netiquette rules?

⬜ Linking Concepts

EXERCISE 33 **Writing in your reading journal**

Answer the following questions in your journal:

1. What is the difference between having a conversation with someone and communicating through e-mail or chat rooms?

2. Why is etiquette important for both ways of communication?

3. Have you ever accidentally broken an etiquette rule?

4. How do you feel when you break a rule?

5. How do you feel when other people don't use good manners toward you?

▭ Assessing Your Learning at the End of the Chapter

Revisiting Chapter Objectives

Return to the first page of this chapter to revisit the chapter objectives. Put a check mark next to the objectives you feel confident about. Review the chapter material you need to learn better. When you are ready, answer the chapter review questions in Exercise 34. These items reflect the chapter objectives and come from all three reading selections.

▭ Practicing for a Chapter Test

EXERCISE 34 **Reviewing comprehension**

Check your comprehension of main concepts, or ideas, in this chapter by answering the following questions. First, write notes to answer the questions without looking back at the readings. Then, use the readings to check your answers and revise them, if necessary. Write your final answers in complete sentences on separate paper.

1. What are some prefixes that mean opposite?
2. Explain the difference between a main idea and a detail in a reading selection. Give an example of a main idea and a detail that supported that main idea you read in this chapter.
3. Write two sentences that are statements of fact and two that are statements of opinion. Explain how you can tell the difference between a fact and an opinion.
4. List as many words or phrases as you can think of that signal that examples will follow.
5. Explain the positive and negative effects of technology.
6. Explain why it is important to think critically about information you find on the Internet.
7. Explain two ways technology has influenced history.

▭ Academic Vocabulary Review

Here are some academic vocabulary words that were introduced in this chapter. Confirm the words whose meanings you know. Identify the words that are not yet part of your active vocabulary. Relearn the words you need to.

1. accommodate	15. computer	29. impact	42. rely
2. accurate	16. conclusion	30. imply	43. research
3. advocate	17. design	31. link	44. revolution
4. aid	18. document	32. logic	45. series
5. appropriate	19. dominate	33. maintain	46. shift
6. assume	20. economic	34. medium	47. site
7. author	21. economy	35. military	48. specific
8. aware	22. encounter	36. negative	49. statistic
9. bias	23. equipment	37. policies	50. subtle
10. challenges	24. equivalent	38. positive	51. technical
11. communicate	25. evaluate	39. prime	52. technological
12. community	26. evidence	40. professionals	53. traffic
13. computations	27. function	41. prospective	54. transform
14. compute	28. ignore		

WEB POWER

You will find additional exercises related to the content in this chapter at **elt.heinle.com/collegereading.**

Answer key for the puzzle

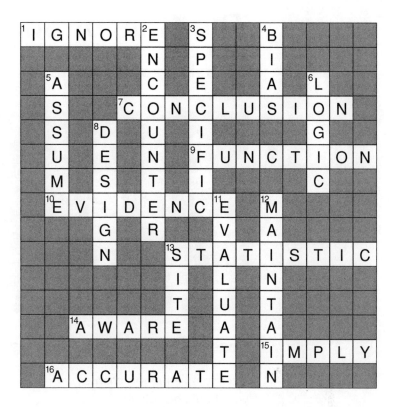

Norms and Values: The Glue of Society

ACADEMIC FOCUS: SOCIOLOGY

Academic Reading Objectives

After completing this chapter, you should be able to:

✓ Check here as you master each objective.

1. Understand new academic vocabulary words ☐
2. Use word parts to guess the meanings of words ☐
3. Recognize the introduction of a scientist's ideas and theories in passages ☐
4. Evaluate the truthfulness of a reading by comparing it with personal experiences ☐
5. Read longer passages more effectively ☐
6. Use a chart to organize reading notes ☐
7. Distinguish main ideas and supporting details ☐

Sociology Objectives

1. Explain what sociologists do ☐
2. Explain how groups affect behavior ☐
3. Define norms and values and explain their relationship ☐
4. Describe people's behavior in group settings ☐
5. Describe Robert Kohl's ideas about American values ☐
6. Compare your values to Kohl's American values ☐

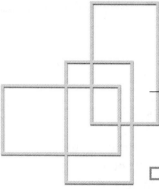

Reading Assignment 1

SOCIOLOGY: STUDYING SOCIETY AND GROUP INFLUENCES

▭ Getting Ready to Read

EXERCISE 1 Participating in class discussion

Before you read Selection 1, discuss the following questions with your classmates.

1. What is sociology?

2. What is the difference between sociology and psychology?

3. What is society?

4. What do sociologists study?

▭ Reading for a Purpose

EXERCISE 2 Noticing special meanings

You probably already know what the word group *means. However, academics sometimes have very specific meanings for words we use in normal conversation. As you read, notice the special meaning of* **group.** *How is it the same as or different from the way you usually use the word? Write your ideas about this on the lines below.*

In this reading, the word "group" means <u>*two or more individuals*</u>

<u>*who. . .*</u>

1. _____

2. _____

3. _____

4. _____

5. _____

Reading Selection 1

SOCIOLOGY: STUDYING SOCIETY AND GROUP INFLUENCES

1   You probably find yourself in different types of social situations every day. Whether you realize it or not, society and the different groups to which you belong have a big impact on you.

What Is a Group?

2   Have you ever said or done something because of the people you were with? If you have, you know that your behavior[1] can be influenced by a group. In sociology, a group is more than just individuals who happen to be in the same place at the same time. To be a group, two or more individuals must:

- Interact with each other.
- Share a common goal.
- Have a relationship that is fairly stable.
- Be interdependent.[2]
- Recognize a relationship among themselves.

---

1. **be•hav•ior** (bĭ-hāv´yər) *n*. The way in which people behave; conduct.
2. **in•ter•de•pen•dent** (ĭn´tər-dĭ-pĕn´dənt) *adj*. Dependent on one another; mutually dependent.

3   You may belong to a number of groups. These groups may include your family, a sports team, a group of friends, a group of co-workers, a religious group, or an after-school club. Each group has certain standards of behavior called norms.

Norms

4   **Norms** are spoken or unspoken rules that tell us how we should behave. They tell us how others expect us to behave. We rely on social norms to help us act appropriately in social situations. For example, while waiting in line to see a movie, we know that others expect us to wait our turn rather than to push to the front of the line.

5   Norms affect how we dress, talk and act. Work norms might require us to dress formally, talk politely, and be punctual.[3] On the other hand, the norms of a social group might include dressing in a current style, using slang,[4] and arriving "fashionably late." Following norms helps keep social interactions running smoothly.

6   You probably follow some norms without realizing it. For instance, when you meet a friend on the street, how do you greet him or her? Do you shake hands? Do you bow? Do you kiss on the cheek? Whatever you do is your norm for greeting friends. This norm may change depending on how well you know the friend. It might be different if the friend is American than if the friend is from another country.

---

3. **punc•tu•al** (pŭngk′chōō-əl) *adj.* Acting or arriving exactly on time; prompt.
4. **slang** (slăng) *n.* A kind of language occurring most often in casual speech, consisting of made-up words and figures of speech deliberately used in place of standard terms to add interest, humor, irreverence, etc.

Norms in Different Cultures

7   Social behavior varies among cultures. This is because different cultures have different social norms. For example, American culture places a high value on being on time. Many other cultures do not think that being on time is so important. Another American value is privacy. Americans enjoy being by themselves. If an American sees someone sitting alone, he or she thinks the person wants privacy. People from another culture might think that person is lonely or sad.

8   When people from different cultures come together, they may experience a "culture clash" because they have different expectations about how people should behave.

Source: Nextext. (2001). *Introduction to Psychology*. Elgin, IL: McDougal Littell, pps. 313–314.

☐ Assessing Your Learning: "Sociology: Studying Society and Group Influences"

Demonstrating Comprehension

EXERCISE 3   **Answering multiple-choice questions**

Circle the letter of the correct response.

1. According to Reading Selection 1, groups can change the way people act.
   a. true   **b.** false

2. According to the definition of the word *group* in paragraph 2, which of the following is a group? Explain why each is or is not a group.
   a. The fans at a basketball game
   b. People on the same bus
   c. Firefighters at a fire station
   d. Guests at a party

3. Norms are
   a. certain standards of behavior.
   b. spoken or unspoken rules.
   c. how others expect us to behave.
   d. all of the above

4. The same person may act differently in one group than in another.
   a. true   **b.** false

5. Norms are the same in all cultures.
   a. true   **b.** false

6. If you see someone sitting alone, that means
   a. that person wants privacy.
   b. that person is sad or lonely.
   c. different things for people of different cultures.
   d. that person is having a culture clash.

7. Culture clashes happen because
   a. some cultures are better than other cultures.
   b. people from different cultures have different norms.
   c. cultures are always changing.
   d. people in some cultures have bad manners.

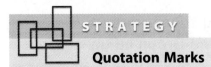

STRATEGY

Quotation Marks

Some words in Reading Selection 1 are in quotation marks " ".
Here are some reasons why writers use quotation marks.

- To show that the words in quotations are the exact words that someone said or wrote
- To show that the words have a special meaning in a sentence
- For titles of magazine articles or short stories

EXERCISE 4   **Understanding quotation marks**

Find the following terms in Reading Selection 1. Discuss with your classmates why the author uses quotation marks.

1. "fashionably late" (¶ 5)
2. "culture clash" (¶ 8)

Learning Vocabulary

EXERCISE 5   **Learning academic words**

These words from Reading Selection 1 are commonly found in academic texts. Study the list of words below, and then learn them by following these guidelines:

1. Number a paper from 1 to 15. Copy these words, leaving space for a definition. Notice that the paragraph location is provided in parentheses next to the word.
2. Write a definition, synonym, or translation for the words you already know.
3. Compare your list with a partner's. Help each other learn new words.
4. Share your list with your classmates. Your instructor can help you define the words you do not know.

1. impact (¶ 1)
2. individuals (¶ 2)
3. interact (¶ 2)
4. goal (¶ 2)
5. stable (¶ 2)
6. team (¶ 3)
7. norms (¶ 3)
8. rely (¶ 4)
9. appropriately (¶ 4)
10. affect (¶ 5)
11. style (¶ 5)
12. interactions (¶ 5)
13. instance (¶ 6)
14. cultures (¶ 7)
15. varies (¶ 7)

Word Parts

You can guess the meanings of some words because a part of one word is similar to a part of another word. For example, the prefix *inter-* means "between two things" or "among many things," so the word international means "between or among nations." An interstate highway is a highway that goes from one state to another.

EXERCISE 6   **Working with word parts**

Find these words in Reading Selection 1. Using the information you know about word parts, write an explanation for each word.

  1. interact (¶ 2) _____

    _____

  2. interdependent (¶ 2) _____

    _____

  3. interactions (¶ 5) _____

    _____

      Here's another word part. The word root *-soci-* has to do with people living, working, or playing together in groups. So, the word *sociable* describes someone who gets along with others or enjoys being a member of a group.

Find these words in Reading Selection 1. Using the information you know about word parts, write an explanation for each word.

  1. sociology (title) _____

    _____

  2. social (¶ 1) _____

    _____

  3. society (¶ 1) _____

    _____

▭ **Focusing on Sociology**

EXERCISE **7** **Understanding norms**

Work in small groups to complete these tasks.

1. Look at paragraphs 3 and 4. In your own words, write a definition for the word **norms.** *Norms are. . .*
2. With your group members, make a list of classroom norms for students and another list of classroom norms for teachers. For example, one classroom norm is for the students to sit at desks. Another norm is for teachers to stand in the front of the class. When you finish, compare your list with those of the whole class.

Norms	
Students	**Teachers**
Sit at desk	*Stand in front*

EXERCISE **8** **Obtaining field experience**

In this exercise, you and your group members will work like sociologists. Sociologists watch how people behave in social situations. From people's behavior, they analyze the norms of the people in those situations. Do the following:

1. With your group members, go to a place where there are several people. (This could be a fast-food restaurant, a mall, or the cafeteria or library in your school.)
2. Observe how people act. Notice role differences.
3. Take notes on people's actions.
4. Combine the notes of all the people in your group.
5. List the norms of the people in the social situations you observed.

▭ **Questions for Review**

EXERCISE 9   Analyzing group memberships

Each of us is a member of several groups. Think about the groups you belong to and how they influence you. You might list one of the groups you belong to as your family, a study group at school, a religious group, and so on.

Groups I belong to	How this group influences me
Family	

Think about the following social situations. Complete the chart by listing the norms for each social situation.

Social situation	Norms
Riding in an elevator	Allow people to get out of the elevator before you get in.
Having a birthday party	
Greeting friends	
Greeting grandparents or elders	
Participating in family meals	
Eating at a restaurant	

▭ **Linking Concepts**

EXERCISE 10   **Writing**

Answer one or all of the following questions:

1. Have you ever experienced a "culture clash"? Describe this experience.

   _____

   _____

   _____

   _____

   _____

   _____

2. What are some norms in your culture that are different from U.S. norms?

   _____

   _____

   _____

   _____

   _____

   _____

3. How does your way of dressing show the group you belong to?

   _____

   _____

   _____

   _____

   _____

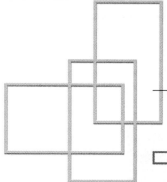

Reading Assignment 2

VALUES AMERICANS LIVE BY

☐ Getting Ready to Read

EXERCISE 11 **Participating in class discussion**

Before you read, discuss the following questions with your classmates:

1. Explain the meaning of these terms:
   a. norms **b.** culture **c.** cultural conflict **d.** values
2. Paragraph 1 of Reading Selection 2 explains the relationship between norms and values. Read the first paragraph. Then, with your classmates, explain the relationship between norms and values.

1 Why do people behave differently? Why do different cultures have different norms? Norms are based on the ideas people see as important in a society. We call the ideas that people think are important values. People show what is important, what they value, by the way they act. So, norms are based on values. For example, some cultures value older people. They believe that people who live a long time have important knowledge. How do they show they value older people? The norm is to treat older people with respect. Young people listen carefully to older people. They help the older people and take care of them. So, a norm of listening to elders with respect is based on the belief that elders are valuable to society.

3. What is culture?
4. How does culture influence norms and values?

☐ Reading for a Purpose

Reading Selection 2 describes the theories of a sociologist named Robert Kohl. Theories are ideas about what an expert believes are true. Each paragraph explains Kohl's ideas.

EXERCISE 12 **Highlighting**

As you read, highlight Kohl's theories. You can find these by looking for the words "According to Kohl . . .", "Kohl says . . .", "Kohl believes . . ." The first one has been done for you as an example.

Reading Selection 2

VALUES AMERICANS LIVE BY

1   Why do people behave differently? Why do different cultures have different norms? Norms are based on the ideas people see as important in a society. We call the ideas that people think are important values. People show what is important, what they value, by the way they act. So, norms are based on values. For example, some cultures value older people. They believe that people who live a long time have important knowledge. How do they show they value older people? The norm is to treat older people with respect. Young people listen carefully to older people. They help the older people and take care of them. So, a norm of listening to elders with respect is based on the belief that elders are valuable to society.

American Culture

2   Robert Kohl is a sociologist. He studies the values of American culture. He uses what he knows about values to help people understand Americans. According to Kohl, it is hard for Americans to explain their values. They think that they are unique individuals. They think each person has his or her own personal values. They believe there are very few values that are common to all Americans. However, Americans are probably not as different as they think.

3   Kohl believes many Americans do not think their values are influenced by society. They think that schools, religion, and family do not impact their values much. It is hard for Americans to see how their values are similar to others. They like to think of themselves as one of a kind. Each person thinks he or she is totally different from anyone else. However, sociologists like Kohl say there are some common American values. They know what these values are because they study the norms of American culture. The way people from any culture act reflects what they value.

Cultural Conflict

4   What causes cultural conflicts? People in one culture behave in a way that is not expected by others. Their actions surprise, insult,[1] or shock others. For example, people in some cultures stand close together when they talk. Standing too close will surprise Americans. It will certainly make them feel uncomfortable.

5   Why is it hard to understand how people act? What people think is important affects the way they act. So, norms (actions) come from what people value (what is important). We can understand "strange" behavior if we understand the values that affect behavior. According to Kohl, there are 13 main American values. These values influence how Americans act. He says that it is important to understand American values. This will help a person to understand 95% of American actions. It can also help to avoid cultural conflicts.

Norms and Values

6   Watch how people act in the United States. Try to see how their actions match with the values on Kohl's list in Reading Selection 3. For example, what is the first question that most Americans ask when they meet someone new? They usually say: "What do you do?" They mean, what is your job? Where do you work? Why is it so important for Americans to know what job you do? This shows the Action/Work value (value 9). Status in American society depends on a person's job. Work is what is valued by Americans. In another country, a more common conversation starter might be: "Tell me about your family." This shows a value of family connections. Family is what determines social status in that country.

1. **in•sult** (ĭn-sŭlt´) *v.* To treat with contempt; offend.

7   Most Americans see the values on Kohl's list as positive. They are not aware that others see these values differently. For example, Americans think "change" (value 2) is a good thing. Americans cannot understand that some cultures see change as negative. Those cultures value tradition. They like to keep things the same. In fact, some other cultures may judge most American values negatively. Kohl says his list of values is not meant to convince people that American values are the best. The list helps others to recognize Americans and their value system.

8   Look at the list of Kohl's values in this chapter. Not all of these values are easy to understand. The next reading explains each value. It also explains how American norms reflect each value. Finally, it compares American values to values of other cultures.

Source: Adapted from Kohl, L. R. (1984). *The Values Americans Live By.* Washington, DC: Meridian House International.

🔲 Assessing Your Learning: "Values Americans Live By"

Demonstrating Comprehension

EXERCISE 13   **Recalling information**

Test your understanding and memory of what you just read. Try to answer these questions without looking at the reading passage. After you answer as many questions as you can, reread the passage and fill in the missing answers.

1. What norms show that young people value older people?

   _____

   _____

   _____

   _____

2. Why is it difficult for Americans to explain their values?

_____

_____

_____

_____

3. What causes cultural conflicts?

_____

_____

_____

_____

4. Why is it important to understand what people value?

_____

_____

_____

_____

5. How do Americans show that work is important?

_____

_____

_____

_____

6. What information will you read about in the next reading passage?

_____

_____

_____

_____

⬛ Learning Vocabulary

EXERCISE 14 **Learning academic words**

These words from Reading Selection 2 are commonly found in academic texts. Look at the list of words below, and then learn them by following these guidelines:

1. Number a paper from 1 to 12. Copy these words, leaving space for a definition. Notice that the paragraph location is provided in parentheses next to the word.
2. Write a definition, synonym, or translation for the words you already know.
3. Compare your list with a partner's. Help each other learn new words.
4. Share your list with your classmates. Your instructor can help you define the words you do not know.

1. sociologist (¶ 2)	**5.** job (¶ 6)	**9.** negative (¶ 7)
2. unique (¶ 2)	**6.** status (¶ 6)	**10.** tradition (¶ 7)
3. individuals (¶ 2)	**7.** positive (¶ 7)	**11.** convince (¶ 7)
4. impact (¶ 3)	**8.** aware (¶ 7)	

EXERCISE 15 **Matching**

Match the academic vocabulary word with the correct meaning.

_____ aware   **1.** position in society, rank

_____ convince   **2.** good

_____ impact   **3.** not positive

_____ individual   **4.** special, different

_____ job   **5.** a person who studies how people act in groups

_____ negative   **6.** work, place of employment

_____ orientation   **7.** tendency, or trend, toward a belief or reaction

_____ positive   **8.** persuade, influence, change someone's mind

_____ sociological   **9.** a custom that is continued for many years

_____ status   **10.** one person

_____ tradition   **11.** know, be conscious of

_____ unique   **12.** influence, effect

▭ Focusing on Sociology

Sociologists try to understand values from different cultures. They do this by observing how the people act. They analyze these actions and make theories about the values of the culture. You can practice working like a sociologist. For the next exercises, work with a group of three or four other students.

EXERCISE 16   **Linking norms and values**

Study the list of norms on the left side of the chart. They describe some norms that can be found in different classrooms. Then make a theory about the values of that classroom. The first one has been done for you as an example.

Classroom norms	Values
1. Students are working together as a group to find the answers to a problem.	*Cooperation and group work*
2. Students sit quietly and listen to the teacher speak.	
3. The teacher has rules about arriving late. The teacher and students in the class are upset when a student arrives late.	
4. The teacher does not accept late homework.	
5. Very strict rules in the class stop students from cheating on tests.	
6. Students call the teacher by her or his first name.	
7. Students send e-mail messages to each other and to their teacher when they are not in class.	

EXERCISE 17   **Linking more norms and values**

Go back to Exercise 7 (after the first reading in this chapter). It was the field experience group project in which you observed the norms of people in a social situation. In the following chart, like the one above, write the norms you observed for the group project on the left side. Write the values that go with those norms on the right side.

Group project norms	Values

⬚ Questions for Review

Robert Kohl, a sociologist, is an expert on values. Still, his theories are just ideas. They are based on his experiences and observations. Look at Kohl's ideas you highlighted in Reading Selection 2. According to your experiences, do you agree with Kohl? Why or why not

_____

_____

_____

EXERCISE 18   Linking theories to personal experience

Fill in the chart below with the specific phrases you highlighted and your opinion. Write Agree *by Kohl's theories you agree with. Write* Disagree *by the theories you do not agree with. Then, compare your Agree and Disagree answers with those of your classmates. Explain why you agree or disagree. Use examples from your own experiences with American culture to help you explain why you agree or disagree.*

Parts you highlighted	Agree or disagree
1. . . . it is hard for Americans to explain their values.	

▭ Linking Concepts

EXERCISE 19   Writing in your reading journal

Answer one or all of the following questions in your journal.

1. Describe one of your personal values. What personal actions show that this is your value?
2. Do you think Americans have a value of respect for older people? Describe how Americans act to show that they respect older people or do not respect older people.
3. Describe what you have learned from observing people's norms in different social situations.

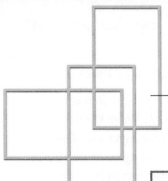

Reading Assignment 3

☐ Getting Ready to Read

STRATEGY

Tips for Reading Longer Selections

1. **Preview the reading selection.** Look at the illustrations. Read the subtitles. Try to get an idea of what the passage is about.

2. **Guess how long it will take you to read.** This will help you plan your time. When you finish reading, check your guess. Did you read it faster or slower than your guess?

3. **Break the reading selection into parts.** Reading Selection 3 is divided into parts by Kohl's list of American values. If you think of each part as a short reading selection, it will be easier to read.

4. **Find a quiet place to read.** You will be able to focus better if you read in a quiet place with good lighting. If there is no quiet place in your home, go to the library or another quiet place.

5. **Use a highlighting marker.** As you read, mark important ideas with a highlighting marker. This will help you focus on the reading and make it easier to review the reading selection later.

☐ Reading for a Purpose

EXERCISE 20   Understanding the terminology of values

Look at Kohl's list of American values below. This list is complex and hard to understand. Circle the values you think you already understand. As you read, compare what you think you understand to Kohl's ideas.

In this reading, Kohl explains thirteen American values. According to Kohl, Americans value:

1. Personal control over the environment
2. Change
3. Time and its control
4. Equality

5. Individualism
6. Self-help
7. Competition
8. Future outlook
9. Action/Work

10. Informality
11. Directness
12. Practicality
13. Materialism

Reading Selection 3

AMERICAN VALUES

1. Personal Control over the Environment

1   Americans do not believe in the power of fate.[1] They do not think that destiny[2] or nature or God controls what happens to them. They believe that they can control their lives. They are responsible for taking control of what happens to them. They do not believe that people's problems are because of bad luck. They believe that people have problems because they are lazy or they do not care.

1. **fate** (fāt) *n.* A force or power that is believed to control events.
2. **des•ti•ny** (dĕs′tə-nē) *n.* The fortune or fate of a person or thing considered inevitable or necessary.

2   In the United States, people consider it normal and right for humans to control nature. People believe every single individual should control the environment. That is why Americans build big dams[3] to keep rivers from flooding.[4] They heat and air-condition their houses. This is a way of controlling the weather. They build roads through mountains. They build "earthquake-proof" buildings. Most Americans find it hard to accept that there are some things that are beyond the power of humans to control.

2. Change

3   For Americans, change is good. Change is linked to improvement, progress, and growth. A good example of this is how Americans work. They often change jobs. Sometimes they change jobs to get more money. However, sometimes they change jobs because they are bored. They just need change.

4   More traditional cultures consider change a disruptive, destructive force. Instead of change, such societies value stability, tradition, and heritage.[5] None of these are valued much in the United States.

3. Time and Its Control

5   For most Americans, time is very important. Often, Americans are more concerned about time than people. It seems impolite when they cut off a discussion to get to their next meeting on time. Americans plan their time carefully. It seems like clocks control them.

6   International visitors soon learn that it is not polite to be late. These people usually come from cultures where human interaction is more important than time. Americans value time because they believe people can accomplish more if they do not "waste" time.

4. Equality

7   Equality is an important American value. Americans say all people are "created equal." Most believe all humans are alike. All people have potential. Everyone has a chance to succeed. For that reason, the American education system is open. Even a college education is open to all people.

---

3. **dam** (dăm) *n.* Barriers across waterways to control the flow or raise the level of water.
4. **flood·ing** (flŭd´ĭng) *v.* Filling or overflowing.
5. **her·i·tage** (hĕr´ĭ-tĭj) *n.* Something other than property passed down from preceding generations.

8   People from some other cultures find equality strange. For some, rank and status are valued. In these cultures, social classes are divided. People in these cultures know their level in society.

9   However, Americans do not treat people of high social status differently from others. This insults many foreign visitors. Even service people treat all people the same. Waiters, clerks, and taxi drivers deal with people similarly. They do not recognize people of different social status. Foreigners to the United States should realize Americans are not trying to be impolite. Visitors should be prepared to be "just like anybody else."

5. Individualism

10   In the United States, each individual is seen as completely unique. Everyone is different from all others. Kohl says that Americans think they are more individualistic in their actions than they are. They don't like to be considered part of a group. They believe they're just a little different from other members of any group they join.

11   Privacy[6] is one effect of individualism. This is difficult for people from other cultures to understand. The word privacy does not even exist in many languages. If it does, it usually has a negative meaning. It means loneliness. In the United States, privacy is very positive. It is common for Americans to say, "If I don't have time to myself, I will go crazy."

6. **pri•va•cy** (prī′və-sē) *n.* The condition of being left alone.

6. Self-Help

12   In the United States, people are proud of their accomplishments.[7] It is important to do things by yourself. People who have an easy life because their parents are rich are not valued as much as those who make their own money. Americans are proud if they climb the ladder of success by themselves. The American social system is open. It makes it possible for Americans to move up the social ladder.[8] Other countries have social systems that discourage people from moving to a higher social status.

13   The value of self-help affects how Americans think about people. They celebrate poor people who work hard. They cheer[9] for people who overcome difficulties. Abraham Lincoln is a good example of this. He was born very poor. He did not have much formal schooling, but he taught himself law. Then he became a lawyer, a politician, and finally president of the United States. Through his hard work he became important.

7. Competition

14   Americans believe that competition makes people better. It brings out the best in people. They believe that people work harder when they are trying to be better than others. Americans compete in many areas. They compete in the arts, education, and sports. Americans feel that when people compete, it makes society better.

15   Some people do not agree with the value of competition. Those people come from cultures that value cooperation. Cooperation means working together, helping each other. For example, they believe children should learn how to work together to solve a problem in school. For them, cooperation is better than one person being the best.

7. **ac•com•plish•ment** (ə-kŏm′plĭsh-mənt) *n.* Acts of completing or carrying out something.
8. **so•cial lad•der** (sō′shəl lăd′ər) *n.* The way people move between lower and higher social status.
9. **cheer** (chîr) *intr.v.* To shout in happiness, approval, encouragement, or enthusiasm.

8. Future Outlook

16   Americans value progress and the future. Not much value is placed on the past. Even if they are happy right now, Americans are hopeful that the future will be better. A lot of energy is focused on a better future. Americans are always planning for the future and setting goals.

17   People from some cultures cannot understand this. This is especially true of cultures with very old traditions. These people are focused on keeping their traditions. Other people have a problem with the future orientation for other reasons. They think it is useless to plan for the future. They believe that their future is controlled by fate.

9. Action/Work

18   Americans say, "Don't just stand there, do something!" For most Americans, action is better than inaction. They usually plan an active day. Even relaxation is preplanned. The main reason to relax is so that you can work harder after relaxing. Even when they go on vacation, activities are carefully planned. People think that it is harmful to "sit around doing nothing," or "just daydream."

19   The action/work orientation has created "workaholics." Workaholics are people who are addicted to their work. They always think about their jobs and are frustrated if they cannot work.

20   People from other cultures value relaxing and personal interactions more. They cannot understand why Americans think their work is so important. They see the value in just "being" without "doing."

10. Informality

21   Someone who comes from another culture will find Americans very informal. They might think Americans are not respectful. Americans are very casual. For example, American bosses often ask their employees to call them by their first names. Some bosses feel uneasy if they are called "Mr. White" or "Mrs. Jones." They like to be called "Donald" or "Kim."

22   An important official from another country will probably find this informality upsetting. On the other hand, an American considers informality a compliment. It shows that people are trying to be friendly. It is not meant to be an insult.

11. Directness

23   For many cultures, it is impolite to say something directly. This is especially true if the information is unpleasant. Americans prefer to be honest. They say things directly. They think that people who are not direct are trying to hide something. They believe indirect people might not be honest. They may distrust anyone who gives hints about something rather than saying it directly.

24   Some people are shocked by Americans' directness. Someone who comes from a country where indirectness is the norm will not be comfortable with Americans.

12. Practicality

25   Americans are usually practical. They believe everything should be useful. The question, How useful is this? is important in every decision. Americans are proud that they are not very idealistic[10] or romantic.

26   Will it make any money? Will it "pay its own way"? What can I get from this? These are the kinds of questions that Americans ask. They don't usually ask questions like: Does it look nice? Will it be enjoyable? Will it increase my knowledge?

27   The love of "practicality" has also caused Americans to see some jobs as better than others. Studying business is much more popular in the United States than philosophy. Law and medicine more valued than the arts.

10. **i•de•al•is•tic** (ī-dē′ə-lĭs′tĭk) *adj.* Believing in principles and high standards even if they cannot be achieved.

13. Materialism

28   Americans are materialistic. This means that they collect more "things" than most people. It also means they value getting, keeping, and protecting their material objects. Sometimes these things are more important than their relationships with people.

29   The modern American typically owns:

- one or more color television sets
- a DVD or video tape player
- stereo system
- a clothes washer and dryer
- a refrigerator, a stove, and a dishwasher
- one or more cars
- a computer
- a mobile phone

30   Americans value newness. They often sell or throw away the things they own and replace them with newer ones. A car may be kept for only two or three years. A house might be kept for five or six before trading it in for another one.

Source: Adapted from Kohl, L. R. (1984). *The Values Americans Live By.* Washington, DC: Meridian House International.

▭ Assessing Your Learning: American Values

Demonstrating Comprehension

EXERCISE 21 Contrasting values

Now that you understand each of these thirteen values separately, look at them in list form (on the left in the chart). Then consider them contrasted with the values of some other countries (on the right in the chart). Check your understanding of the other values listed on the right. Look up unfamiliar words in a dictionary, and discuss the meaning contrasts with your classmates.

U.S. values		Other countries' values
Control over environment		Fate
Change		Tradition
Time & its control		Human interaction
Equality		Different social status
Individualism		Group benefit
Self-help		Heritage
Competition		Cooperation
Future orientation		Past orientation
Work orientation		Relaxing/social interaction
Informality		Formality
Directness		Indirectness
Practicality/Efficiency		Idealism/romanticism
Materialism		Nonmaterialism

The ideas presented in "American Values" are taken from a psychology book. One way to remember what you read in textbooks is to take notes on the reading selection. Have you taken notes on a reading selection before? How did you organize your notes? One strategy that can help you understand and remember difficult texts is to organize the information. The **chart** in Exercise 22 shows one way to organize the information in this reading.

EXERCISE 22 Organizing reading notes in a chart

Complete the chart as shown. The first value from Reading Selection 3 has been done for you as an example.

Values	Norms	Other countries' values	My experiences
1. Personal control over the environment	Control nature by building dams, heating, air conditioning, etc.	Fate, destiny	Air-conditioned cars
2.			
3.			
4.			
5.			
6.			
7.			
8.			
9.			
10.			
11.			
12.			
13.			

STRATEGY

Supporting Details

Supporting details are the sentences in a passage that explain the different points of the main idea. There are two types of supporting details: major and minor, sometimes called primary and secondary. Major details directly develop the main idea; minor details exemplify further the major details. It is important to notice transitions from main ideas to details when you read.

To better understand detail relationships, consider the sequence illustrated below:

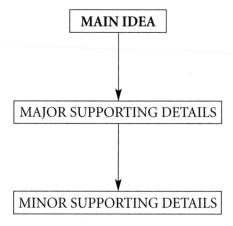

Supporting details are often, but not always, introduced by signal words. These signals can help a reader distinguish organizational patterns. Supporting details provide the reader with additional information that describes, illustrates, or explains why, when, and how something happened. These details might also include data or statistics, steps in a process, and examples of what is being talked about. It is important to be able to distinguish supporting details from the main idea because the details are very specific. In addition, supporting details are clues to finding patterns of organization. If you can picture a house, the roof is the main idea and the walls are the supporting details.

EXERCISE 23   **Recognizing main ideas and supporting details**

Here are two paragraphs from the reading selections to analyze for main ideas and details. The first one is done for you as an example. The second one is for you to analyze.

1. For Americans, change is good. Change is linked to improvement, progress, and growth. A good example of this is how Americans work. They often change jobs. Sometimes they change jobs to get more money. However, sometimes they change jobs because they are bored. They just need change.

   Analysis: *This paragraph is about Americans and change. Sentence number 1 is the main idea. The next sentence tells why Americans think change is good. In the third sentence, "work" is given an example. This is a major support. The next sentences are minor support. They give more details about changing jobs and why.*

2. Social behavior varies among cultures. This is because different cultures have different social norms. For example, American culture places a high value on being on time. Many other cultures do not think that being on time is so important. Another American value is privacy. Americans enjoy being by themselves. If an American sees someone sitting alone, they think the person wants privacy. People from another culture might think that person is lonely or sad.

   Analysis: *This paragraph is about* _____

   _____

   _____

   _____

   _____

   _____

   _____

   _____

   _____

Here is a list of markers and signal words that often introduce supporting details.

Function	Signal words
Addition	and, also, too, in addition, moreover, another
Cause/effect	as a result, since, therefore, because, consequently, for that reason
Chronology/sequence	all time expressions, first, second, after, next
Classification/listing	A, B, C, 1, 2, 3, • • • •
Contrast/opposition/surprise	in contrast, on the other hand, however, nevertheless, instead of, even
Definition	i.e. , that is, this is, ( ), —
Example	e.g., for example, such as, for instance, to demonstrate
Process	first, second, next, then

These words are important to notice when you're reading because they signal supporting details.

EXERCISE 24 Identifying main ideas and supporting details

Read the following sentences taken from Reading Selection 3. Write MI next to main ideas. Write SD next to supporting details.

1. __MI__ For Americans, change is a good.

2. _____ A good example of this is how Americans work.

3. _____ Instead of change, such societies value stability, tradition, and heritage.

4. _____ Equality is an important American value.

5. _____ For that reason, the American education system is open.

6. _____ In the United States, people are proud of their accomplishments.

7. _____ Abraham Lincoln is a good example of this.

8. _____ Then he became a lawyer, a politician, and finally president of the United States.

9. _____ Some people do not agree with the value of competition.

10. _____ For example, they believe children should learn how to work together to solve a problem in school.

11. _____ For most Americans, action is better than inaction.

12. _____ Even when they go on vacation, activities are carefully planned.

13. _____ For many cultures, it is impolite to say something directly.

14. _____ This is especially true if the information is unpleasant.

Go back to each sentence and circle the signal word(s) in the supporting details.

▭ Learning Vocabulary

Learning academic words

These words from Reading Selection 3 are commonly found in academic texts. Study the list of words below, and then learn them by following these guidelines:

1. Number a paper from 1 to 16. Copy these words, leaving space for a definition. The paragraph location is provided in parentheses next to the word.
2. Write a definition, synonym, or translation for the words you already know.
3. Compare your list with a partner's. Help each other learn new words.
4. Share your list with your classmates. Your instructor can help you define the words you do not know.

1. environment (¶ 2)
2. individualism (¶ 11)
3. normal (¶ 2)
4. linked (¶ 3)
5. stability (¶ 4)
6. created (¶ 7)
7. potential (¶ 7)
8. areas (¶ 14)
9. cooperation (¶ 15)
10. finally (¶ 13)
11. energy (¶ 16)
12. relaxation (¶ 18)
13. idealistic (¶ 25)
14. philosophy (¶ 27)
15. tape (¶ 29)
16. computer (¶ 29)

Using academic vocabulary

Sometimes it is easy to remember new words if you know the opposite of the word. Look at the academic word list. Find the word from the academic word list that is the opposite of each word below. Write the word beside its opposite.

1. practical _____
2. destroyed _____
3. competition _____
4. strange _____
5. conformity _____
6. firstly _____
7. unrelated _____

EXERCISE 27   **Using the right words**

Write the word from the academic word list that best completes the following sentences.

1. _____ is important when working with a team of people.

2. Americans do not like to waste time or _____.

3. The natural _____ includes the plants and animals around us.

4. He could be someone great; he has a lot of _____.

5. In the contest, participants compete in many _____.

6. Vacation is a time of _____.

7. Ancient Greeks were famous for developing _____.

8. The value that one person is different or unique is called _____.

9. He _____ got to the last problem.

10. The opposite of realistic is _____.

11. Since the speech was interesting, they saved it on a _____.

12. It is _____ to think that all people are good.

13. Bad nutrition is _____ to disease.

14. I now have a _____. I can send you e-mail.

15. For a balanced life, people need _____.

⬜ Focusing on Sociology

EXERCISE 28   **Placing yourself on a continuum of values**

After reading Kohl's ideas about American values, think about your own values. Below is a chart showing U.S. values compared with some other countries' values. Are your values more like American values or like others' values?

- *Think about each pair of values.*
- *Make an X in the box by the value that reflects how you feel. For example, if you believe fate controls your life, make an X near "Fate." If you believe humans can control the environment, make an X near "Control over Environment." If you believe both are equally important, make an X in the center of "Neutral."*
- *Repeat this for each of the other twelve values.*

U.S. values	X More like me	X Neutral	X More like me	Other countries' values
Control over environment				Fate
Change				Tradition
Time & its control				Human interaction
Equality				Different social status
Individualism				Group benefit
Self-help				Heritage
Competition				Cooperation
Future outlook				Past outlook
Work				Relaxing/Social interaction

You will often have to remember the important points from material you are assigned to read. Sometimes it is difficult to remember what you have read. Here are some strategies to help you remember what you have read. Try one or all of them.

1. Recite what you have read right after you finish.

2. Try to make a connection to something you already know. For example, you may have an American friend who has a new car. You can think of this and remember that Americans are often materialistic—they value things like cars.

3. Think of the illustrations that go with the reading selection.

U.S. values	X More like me	X Neutral	X More like me	Other countries' values
Informal				Formal
Direct				Indirect
Practical/efficient				Idealistic/romantic
Materialistic				Nonmaterialistic

▭ Questions for Review

EXERCISE 29   Working to remember what you have learned

Try these two memory tests.

1. *How many of Kohl's thirteen values can you remember? Without looking back at the reading, write down as many of the values as you can remember. When you can't remember any more, look back at the reading selection to compare.* I can remember these values. . .

   1.

   2.

   3.

2. *Think of the six pictures that go with the reading selection. Close your eyes and try to "see" the pictures and the words on the page. Write down the first three you remember. Then compare the points you remember with a partner's.*
   I can remember pictures of. . .

   1.

   2.

   3.

▭ Linking Concepts

EXERCISE 30 Writing in your reading journal

Write about one or all of these topics in your reading journal:

1. Choose one personal value. Explain how you are similar to or different from Americans in this value.

2. Reading Selection 1 was about how groups influence the way we think and act. What groups have influenced your values? Explain.

3. Usually, norms are reflected by what people value. However, sometimes there is a difference between what people say they value and how they act. For example, according to Kohl, equality is an American value. At the same time, not everyone is treated equally in the United States. In some places, people of different nationalities or races are treated badly. What do you think about this? Can you think of other examples of how American norms sometimes do not reflect what they say they value?

▭ Assessing Your Learning at the End of a Chapter

Revisiting Objectives

Return to the first page of this chapter to revisit the chapter objectives. Put a check mark next to the objectives you feel confident about. Review the material in the chapter you need to learn better. When you are ready, take the practice test on the next page. These items reflect the chapter objectives and come from all three reading selections.

Practicing for a Chapter Test

EXERCISE 31 Reviewing comprehension

Assess your learning of important points from this chapter by answering the following questions:

1. List three phrases you might read that introduce a person's ideas or theories.

2. What are three things you can do to read long reading passages more effectively?

3. What are some things you can do to help you remember what you have read?

4. How are main ideas different from supporting details?

5. What is sociology? What do sociologists do?

6. How do groups affect people's behavior?

7. Define *norms* and *values* and explain how they are related.

8. How do sociologists decide what the norms of different cultures are?

9. What does *cultural conflict* mean?

10. According to Robert Kohl, why is it important for people from other countries to understand American values?

▭ Academic Vocabulary Review

On the next page are some academic vocabulary words that were introduced in this chapter. Confirm the words whose meaning you know. Identify the words that are not yet part of your active vocabulary. Relearn the words you need to.

The following pair activity can help you study these vocabulary words with your classmates.

1. Each pair is responsible for different words on the list. Your instructor will give each pair a note card for each of your words.

2. With your partner, write definitions for each of your words on a different note card in your own words. If you are unsure of the meaning, reread the text and try to guess the meaning. Both you and your partner must agree to the wording of the definition.

3. Pass your note cards to another pair.

4. When you receive note cards from another group, try to match each note card to a word on the list.

5. After you have done all the note cards for all the pairs, discuss which definitions were clear and which could be improved. Suggest how the definitions could be improved.

1. affect	10. energy	19. instance	28. philosophy	37. style
2. appropriately	11. environment	20. interact	29. positive	38. tape
3. areas	12. finally	21. interactions	30. potential	39. team
4. aware	13. focused	22. job	31. relaxation	40. tradition
5. computer	14. goal	23. linked	32. rely	41. unique
6. convince	15. idealistic	24. negative	33. sociologist	42. varies
7. cooperation	16. impact	25. normal	34. stability	
8. created	17. individualism	26. norms	35. stable	
9. cultures	18. individuals	27. orientation	36. status	

WEB POWER

You will find additional exercises related to the content
in this chapter at **elt.heinle.com/collegereading.**

The Attraction of Diamonds

ACADEMIC FOCUS: GEOLOGY

The 44.5-carat Hope Diamond

Academic Reading Objectives

After completing this chapter,
you should be able to:

✓ Check here as you
master each objective.

1. Make predictions about text ☐
2. Recognize words that mark time sequence ☐
3. Answer comprehension questions about reading text ☐
4. Use new vocabulary ☐
5. Draw conclusions from information ☐
6. Make connections between personal experiences
   and texts ☐
7. Synthesize ideas from differenct reading sources ☐

Science Objectives

1. Take notes using a graphic organizer ☐
2. Compare information from different texts ☐
3. Prepare for tests by explaining a process orally ☐

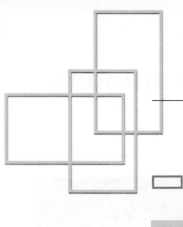

Reading Assignment 1

THE CURSE OF THE HOPE DIAMOND

☐ Getting Ready to Read

EXERCISE 1 **Participating in class discussion**

Discuss the following items with your classmates:

1. Use a dictionary. Look up the word *curse*. What is a curse?
2. Write the definition of *curse*.

   _____.

3. Do you think things can be cursed?
4. Can you give an example of something that is cursed?
5. Have you ever heard of the Hope Diamond?
6. Why are diamonds considered so valuable?

EXERCISE 2 **Making predictions**

One way to improve your reading is to guess what the text is about. This helps you focus on the topic. This kind of guessing is called making predictions.

Complete these two activities before you read on:

1. Look at the pictures. Guess what this reading passage is about.

   From the pictures, I think that maybe _____

   _____

   _____

2. The title of this selection is "The Curse of the Hope Diamond." Guess what kinds of things might have happened to owners of the Hope Diamond.

   From the title, I think that maybe _____

   _____

   _____

☐ Reading the Selection

STRATEGY

Time Order

Academic textbooks can be organized in many ways. "The Curse of the Hope Diamond" is organized in time order. The events are presented in the order they happened in time. Here are some words that show time order:

- first, second, third, etc.
- before, next, after, later, etc.
- in the end, finally, at last, etc.

EXERCISE 3 Noticing time order expressions

As you read this selection, underline the words that show time order.

Reading Selection 1

THE CURSE OF THE HOPE DIAMOND

The Hindu
goddess Sita

Marie Antoinette

1   The 44.5-carat Hope Diamond is the world's largest blue diamond. It is also one of the most popular attractions in the Smithsonian National Museum of Natural History in Washington, D.C. The Hope Diamond is flawless[1] and priceless. However, ownership of this gem has not always been a stroke of great fortune.

2   The Hope Diamond is a remnant[2] of a 112-carat Indian diamond stolen from a statue of the Hindu goddess Sita. The angry goddess cast a spell of misfortune on anyone who acquired the gem. The spell began to work when the stone arrived in France. It was sold to the French King, Louis XIV. Louis had the gem cut into a 67-carat jewel. After wearing it once, he became sick and died of smallpox.[3] Next, the stone passed down to Louis XVI and his wife, Marie Antoinette. Their bad misfortune was to lose their heads in the French Revolution.

1. **flaw•less** (flô′lĭs) *adj.* Without any defect; perfect.
2. **rem•nant** (rĕm′nənt) *n.* A portion left over; a remainder, what is left.
3. **small•pox** (smôl′pŏks′) *n.* A serious, often fatal, highly infectious disease with symptoms that include pimples that develop into pockmarks.

3   The gem was stolen again at the end of the French Revolution. It reappeared in London 38 years later. It was recut and bought by a British banker and gem collector, Henry Thomas Hope. We do not know about any misfortune Henry Hope suffered. However, in 1890 Lord Francis Hope inherited the Hope Diamond. His wife soon ran off with another man. Lord Hope was later forced to sell the diamond to avoid bankruptcy.[4] His unfaithful wife died in poverty.

4   The ongoing woeful[5] story of the diamond's owners continued for decades. An Eastern European prince gave it to an exotic dancer.[6] But later he became jealous and shot her to death. Another owner had a car accident and died with his wife and children. Finally, in 1911, Evalyn Walsh McLean purchased the Hope Diamond. She was a wealthy American socialite.[7] She was sometimes unconventional. For example, she had her Great Dane[8] wear the diamond to greet party guests. She said she did not believe in the diamond's curse. However, she suffered several personal tragedies while she owned the gem. Her son died in a car accident. Her daughter died from an overdose of sleeping pills, and her husband went insane.

Evalyn Walsh McLean

5   The diamond's final owner, Harry Winston, bought the stone after Dame McLean died in 1947. He donated it to the Smithsonian 11 years later. Without explaining his actions, Winston sent the stone in a plain brown wrapper to the museum. The Hope Diamond now holds a place of honor in the museum's remodeled Hall of Gems, perhaps bringing an end to its colorful yet sometimes tragic history.

Source: Adapted from Chernicoff, S. (1999). *Geology: An Introduction to Physical Geology* (2nd ed.). Boston: Houghton Mifflin Company, p. 59.

4. **bank•rupt•cy** (băngk′rəpt-sē) *n.* Being completely without money.
5. **woe•ful** (wō′fəl) *adj.* Full of woe; mournful; deeply unhappy.
6. **ex•ot•ic danc•er** (ĭg-zŏt′ĭk dăns′ər) *n.* An entertainer whose performance consists of slowly removing her or his clothing, usually to musical accompaniment.
7. **so•cial•ite** (sō′shə-līt′) *n.* A person who is prominent in fashionable society.
8. **Great Dane** (grāt dān) *n.* A type of dog having a short smooth coat and a narrow head.

☐ Assessing Your Learning: The Curse of the Hope Diamond

Demonstrating Comprehension

EXERCISE **4** **Checking predictions**

How well did you predict what the reading selection was about? Which predictions were correct? Which predictions were not correct?

EXERCISE **5** **Connecting events**

Reread the selection. Complete the "chain of events" on the next page as you read. Write the names of the owners in the diamond-shaped boxes. Put the "curse" of each owner in the connecting box. Some parts of the "Chain of Events" have been completed as an example. Check your Chain of Events with your instructor.

EXERCISE **6** **Making logical guesses**

Sometimes we can make a guess about information even though it is not stated exactly in the text. Answer the following questions based on guesses you can make from the text.

1. The last sentence in paragraph 2, "Their bad misfortune was to lose their heads in the French Revolution," means
   a. Louis XIV and Marie Antoinette went crazy.
   b. Louis XIV and Marie Antoinette were executed.
   c. Louis XIV and Marie Antoinette were always having bad luck.
   d. Louis XIV and Marie Antoinette lost the French Revolution.

2. The original diamond was 112 carats, but the present diamond is 44.5 carats because
   a. it was cut only once by Louis XIV into a smaller diamond.
   b. when diamonds get older some of the carats disappear.
   c. it was cut at least twice.
   d. it was lost during the French Revolution.

3. Why was Dame McLean considered unconventional?
   a. She mailed the diamond in a plain brown wrapper.
   b. She let her dog wear the Hope Diamond.
   c. She suffered many family tragedies.
   d. She donated the diamond to the Smithsonian Institution.

4. The Hope Diamond finally ended up
   a. in France.
   b. in England.
   c. in India.
   d. in the United States.

5. In the last sentence, "The Hope Diamond now holds a place of honor in the museum's remodeled Hall of Gems, *perhaps* bringing an end to its colorful yet sometimes tragic history"; the word *perhaps* is in *italics* because
   a. it is a difficult word to understand.
   b. the author thinks the Hope Diamond may still have a curse.
   c. the Hope Diamond's place of honor might be replaced by another, more famous gem.
   d. the author believes the gem wasn't always colorful and tragic.

▭ Focusing on Science

Hope Diamond Chain of Events

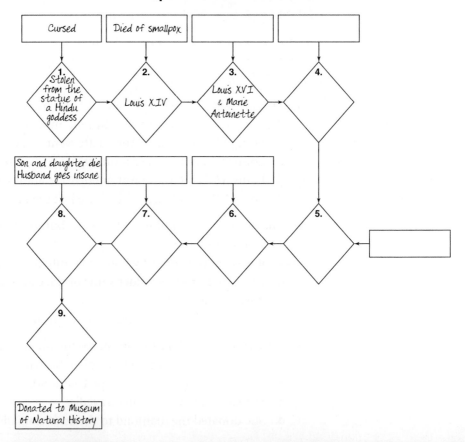

▭ Learning Vocabulary

EXERCISE 7   **Studying academic vocabulary**

These words from the reading selection are commonly found in academic texts. Study the list of words below, and then learn them by following these guidelines:

1. Number a paper from 1 to 10. Copy these words, leaving spaces for definitions. The paragraph location is provided in parentheses next to the word.
2. Write a definition, synonym, or translation for each word you already know.
3. Compare your list with a partner's. Help each other learn new words.
4. Share your list with your classmates. Your instructor can help you define the words you do not know.

1. fortune (¶ 1)
2. acquired (¶ 2)
3. misfortune (¶ 2)
4. revolution (¶ 2)
5. avoid (¶ 3)

6. ongoing (¶ 4)
7. decade (¶ 4)
8. purchase (¶ 4)
9. unconventional (¶ 4)
10. final (¶ 5)

Match each vocabulary word with a word that can follow it in a sentence.

1. acquired _____
2. avoid _____
3. ongoing _____
4. purchased _____
5. unconventional _____
6. final _____

a. story
b. the diamond
c. socialite
d. bankruptcy
e. owner
f. gem

EXERCISE **8**   **Filling in the blanks**

Complete the following story with the correct academic vocabulary words.

Henry's Big Business Mistake

For ten years Henry was a successful businessman. In fact, for a

(1) _____ he had a normal, **(2)** _____

business that provided office supplies to other businesses. Henry was

very successful. But then, **(3)** _____ struck his business.

Important changes occurred in the way businesses worked. It was a

business **(4)** _____. Businesses that used to

(5) _____ supplies from Henry became more computerized.

They did not use the same kinds of supplies. Now they were using more

electronic equipment and less paper.

Henry's business had not changed with the times. Fortunately he

was able to **(6)** _____ going out of business by changing

the types of products he sold. His business also **(7)** _____

new computers, and Henry got training for his employees. The

(8) _____ result is that Henry learned an important lesson.

A successful businessman must keep up with the **(9)** _____

changes that take place. If he wants to keep his good **(10)** _____,

he must be prepared for the future.

POWER GRAMMAR

Noticing How Words Are Used

A word can have more than one meaning. To know what a word
means, you must read the sentence the word is in. For example, you
might know that the word *spell* means to write words with the correct
letters, but *spell* has other meanings too. In the case of writing words
correctly, the word *spell* is used as a verb.

EXERCISE 9 Studying words with more than one meaning

Find these words in Reading Selection 1 as noted, and select the correct meanings.

1. Find the word *spell* in the first paragraph. What does *spell* mean in paragraph 1?
   a. a period of time   **b.** a curse   **c.** to give someone a break

2. Find the word *cut* in the second paragraph. What does *cut* mean in paragraph 2?
   a. divide into pieces   **b.** shape a gem   **c.** edit   **d.** stop

---

POWER GRAMMAR

Word Parts

Affixes are word parts that go together to build words. If you know the meanings of the affixes, you can sometimes guess the meanings of words. For example, the affix *pre-* means "before" or "beginning," so a **pre**fix is the beginning of a word, and **pre**view means to look at something quickly before you look at it carefully.

EXERCISE 10 Noticing affixes

Quickly scan through the reading text again to find these words and circle them.

reappeared	flaw**less**	color**ful**
recut	price**less**	**un**faith**ful**
remodeled	woe**ful**	**un**conventional

Work with a partner. Answer the following questions:

1. What does the prefix *re-* mean?

   _____

2. List at least two more words that begin with the prefix *re-*.

   a. _____

   b. _____

3. What does the suffix *-less* mean?

   _____

4. List at least two more words that end with the suffix *-less*.

   a. _____

   b. _____

5. What does the suffix *-ful* mean?

   _____

6. List at least two more words that end with the suffix *-ful*.

   a. _____

   b. _____

7. What does the prefix *un-* mean?

   _____

8. List at least two more words that begin with the prefix *un-*.

   a. _____

   b. _____

EXERCISE 11   Studying phrasal verbs

Look at Reading Selection 1 again. Find these phrasal verbs and circle them. Guess what they mean. Write your own original sentence with each of these two-word verbs.

Phrasal verbs	Sentences
passed down (¶ 2)	
ran off (¶ 3) (run off)	
believe in (¶ 4)	

☐ Questions for Review

EXERCISE 12 **Answering questions in a small group**

Work with a group of three or four other students. Discuss these two questions:

1. Why do people believe in curses?
2. How does a society help keep curses alive?

Summarize your group discussion, and share your summary with the rest of your classmates.

_____

_____

_____

_____

_____

_____

_____

_____

_____

☐ Linking Concepts

EXERCISE 13 **Writing in your reading journal**

Respond to one or more of these topics in your reading journal:

1. Write your personal answer to one of the questions listed in Exercise 12.
2. What are the two most interesting things you learned from reading this selection?
3. What else would you like to know about the Hope Diamond?

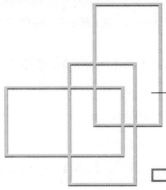

Reading Assignment 2

THE CURSE OF THE HOPE DIAMOND?

☐ Getting Ready to Read

EXERCISE 14 Making predictions

Notice the title and pictures for Reading Selection 2, and make some predictions. Answer these questions before you read.

1. Reading Selection 1 is titled "The Curse of the Hope Diamond." Reading Selection 2 has the same title, but the title ends in a question mark. Why do you think it ends in a question mark?

   Maybe it ends with a question mark because

   _____

2. Predict what this reading selection will be about.

   From the title and pictures, I think that maybe

   _____

EXERCISE 15 Previewing vocabulary and concepts

Discuss the following items with your classmates:

1. **Embellishing a Story**

   A good storyteller adds details or facts to a true story to make it more interesting or exciting, we call this embellishing a story. Can you think of stories that have been embellished? Have you ever embellished a story to make it more interesting or exciting? Reading Selection 2 tells how the story of the curse of the Hope Diamond became embellished.

2. **Superstitions**

   A superstition is a belief in something that is not based on fact. For example, in English-speaking countries, superstitious people believe that black cats and walking under ladders bring bad luck, and that Friday the thirteenth is a day of bad luck. What are some other superstitions?

▭ Reading the Selection

Reading Selection 2 has more information about the curse of the
Hope Diamond. It also includes details different from those in Reading
Selection 1. As you read this selection, notice the new details and different
information.

Reading Selection 2

THE CURSE OF THE HOPE DIAMOND?

1   Is the Hope Diamond really cursed? How did the story of the
diamond's curse get started? Some people believe that the curse
of the Hope Diamond was at least embellished[1] if not invented by
Pierre Cartier. Pierre Cartier sold the diamond to Evalyn Walsh
McLean. This is Evalyn's memory of Pierre Cartier's story as told in
her autobiography,[2] *Father Struck it Rich*:

> We all stared at that diamond. Monsieur Cartier began to tell us
> things about the gem. For example, he said that Tavernier stole
> the gem from a Hindu statue. Because of that, he was cursed
> and torn apart by wild dogs. Since then, the diamond brought
> bad luck to anyone who wore or even touched it. Louis XIV died
> a terrible death from gangrene.[3] We all know about the knife
> blade that cut through Marie Antoinette's throat. Lord Francis
> Hope had plenty of troubles. His wife ran off with handsome
> Captain Strong. Now maybe that was not bad luck, but it was
> embarrassing. Monsieur[4] Cartier was most entertaining.

2   Pierre Cartier himself said of the diamond's curse, "I think,
myself, that superstitions[5] are not based in fact. Yet, one must
admit, they are amusing."[6]

Pierre Cartier

---

1. **em•bel•lished** (ĕm-bĕl´ĭsh) *tr.v.* Added imaginative details to something; made
   beautiful by ornamentation.
2. **au•to•bi•og•ra•phy** (ô´tō-bī-ŏg´rə-fē) *n.* The story of a person's life when written
   by that person.
3. **gan•grene** (găng´grēn´) *n.* Decay of tissue in a living body.
4. **Mon•sieur** (mə-syoe´) *n.* French for *Mister.*
5. **su•per•sti•tion** (soo´pər-stĭsh´ən) *n.* An action or a practice that is based on
   faith, in magic, or on chance.
6. **a•mus•ing** (ə-myoo̅z´ĭng) *adj.* Entertaining.

3   "Pierre Cartier was a clever jeweler. He knew how to sell a diamond," says Jeffrey Post, Curator[7] of the National Gem Collection at the Smithsonian. "The stories of a curse seem to start at about the time Evalyn Walsh McLean bought the diamond. Cartier knew that Evalyn was interested in charms. He probably added the story of a curse. There weren't any references about a curse until that time."

4   "There was also a book that was published in 1921 by May Yohe. She was the wife of Lord Francis Hope. That seems to be the source of a lot of the incredible stories and misinformation about the Hope Diamond. Besides, Evalyn Walsh McLean loved to tell the stories. So the stories just kept growing from a very tiny seed of truth. Once a story starts to grow beyond the truth, it's hard to find the truth. The curse is an interesting part of the story of the Hope Diamond. The curse has helped to make the diamond famous. But as a scientist and a curator, I don't believe in curses."

5   "For example, poor John Baptiste Tavernier was supposedly ripped apart by a pack of wild dogs on his last visit to India. Well, in fact, he made himself quite a fortune selling diamonds to French kings. He lived to an old age and died in Russia."

6   "In his many trips from France to India, Tavernier established a profitable trade relationship with some of India's most powerful rulers. Stealing a gem from a statue of a god doesn't seem like the kind of risk he would've taken. Tavernier made detailed drawings of the stones he traded. His top, bottom, and side views of the large blue stone he brought from India reveal a shape much too flat and irregular to have been used for a statue's eye."

7   "People look at Marie Antoinette," continues Post, "and they say, 'Well, here's another example of what happened to someone who wore this Blue Diamond.' But only the king wore that gem for special ceremonial occasions. Marie Antoinette would never have worn it. Though it could be argued that her husband, King Louis XVI, had some bad luck."

8   "Even Sultan[8] Abdul Hamid II, who owned the diamond before Cartier, lost the Ottoman Empire through bad management, not because of the curse of the diamond. Most of the other stories spread by May Yohe and Cartier are not based in fact."

---

7. **cu•ra•tor** (kyŏŏ-rā′tər) *n.* A person who manages a museum, library, or zoo.
8. **sul•tan** (sŭl′tən) *n.* A ruler of a Muslim country.

9   "Almost monthly I get letters from people who like to think that everything bad that's happened to the United States for the past forty years is because the Hope Diamond now belongs to the United States. Here at the Smithsonian, we've always looked at the Hope Diamond as a source of *good luck*. Since it was given to the Smithsonian, the national gem collection has grown greatly in importance. It really was the gift of the Hope Diamond that made us famous and helped the collection to grow."

10   "People love to believe in curses. As far as Evalyn Walsh McLean is concerned, both the tragedy and the joy of her life added to the story of the curse of the Hope Diamond. She did have a tragic life. For good or for bad, she had a real impact on the Hope Diamond."

Source: Adapted from *Treasures of the World: Stories Behind Masterworks of Art and Nature.* (1999). PBS (Public Broadcasting System) Online

▭ Assessing Your Learning: The Curse of the Hope Diamond?

Demonstrating Comprehension

EXERCISE 16   **Answering comprehension questions**

Answer the following questions based on Reading Selection 2:

1. Did Pierre Cartier believe in the curse of the Hope Diamond? Why or why not?
2. Why did Pierre Cartier tell Evalyn Walsh McLean about the curse of the diamond?
3. Does Jeffery Post think the Hope Diamond is cursed? Explain why he thinks this way.
4. What reasons does Jeffery Post give to support his belief that John Baptiste Tavernier did not steal the diamond from the statue of the goddess?
5. What kind of letters does Jeffery Post receive about the diamond?
6. Do you agree with Jeffery Post's statement "People love to believe in curses"? Explain why you agree or disagree.

EXERCISE 17   Comparing texts

Reread "The Curse of the Hope Diamond?" Complete these charts with new details and different information.

Questions	New details
How did Evalyn Walsh McLean get the diamond?	
How did the diamond come from India to France?	
What did Lord Francis Hope's wife do?	
Who was the Eastern European Prince?	

Information from Reading Selection 1	Different information from Reading Selection 2
The diamond was stolen from the statue of a Hindu goddess.	
Louis XIV died of smallpox.	
Marie Antoinette wore the diamond.	
The diamond is a source of bad luck.	

EXERCISE 18 Contrasting texts

Read the following statements. Write 1 if the information comes from Reading Selection 1, write 2 if the information comes from Reading Selection 2, and write B if it is found in both.

1. _____ The Hope Diamond came from India.

2. _____ John Baptiste Tavernier sold the diamond to King Louis XIV.

3. _____ Marie Antoinette was the wife of King Louis XVI.

4. _____ The diamond was named after Lord Hope of England.

5. _____ Pierre Cartier bought the diamond from Sultan Abdul Hamid II.

6. _____ The diamond was given to an exotic dancer.

7. _____ Evalyn Walsh McLean suffered many tragedies.

8. _____ Evalyn Walsh McLean's husband went insane.

9. _____ The Hope Diamond was donated by Harry Winston.

10. _____ The Hope Diamond is currently in the Smithsonian Institution.

11. _____ The story about the Hope Diamond was embellished.

12. _____ Terrible things happened to those who owned the diamond.

13. _____ The Hope Diamond belongs to the United States.

14. _____ An Eastern European prince owned the diamond.

15. _____ Lord Hope's wife died poor.

⬜ Learning Vocabulary

EXERCISE 19   **Studying academic vocabulary**

These words from Reading Selection 2 are commonly found in academic texts. Study the list of words below, and then learn them by following these guidelines:

1. Number a paper from 1 to 23. Copy these words, leaving spaces for definitions. The paragraph location is provided in parentheses next to the word.
2. Write a definition, synonym, or translation for each word you already know.
3. Compare your list with a partner's. Help each other learn new words.
4. Share your list with your classmates. Your instructor can help you define the words you do not know.

1. throat (¶ 1)
2. plenty (¶ 1)
3. entertaining (¶ 1)
4. admit (¶ 2)
5. charms (¶ 3)
6. references (¶ 3)
7. published (¶ 4)
8. source (¶ 4)

9. misinformation (¶ 4)
10. tiny (¶ 4)
11. supposedly (¶ 5)
12. apart (¶ 5)
13. fortune (¶ 5)
14. established (¶ 6)
15. profitable (¶ 6)
16. trade (¶ 6)

17. powerful (¶ 6)
18. reveal (¶ 6)
19. argued (¶ 7)
20. management (¶ 8)
21. national (¶ 9)
22. collection (¶ 9)
23. impact (¶ 10)

Study List—Example

1. Throat: a body part that is a passage for food, drink, air, and your voice.

2. Plenty:

STRATEGY

Vocabulary Cards

How can you learn new vocabulary words? One way is with flashcards. Use index cards and a dictionary. Look up a word in an English or bilingual dictionary. On one side of a card, write the word you want to remember. On the other side of the card, write the definition of that word or write that word in your first language. Make a card for each word. You can carry your cards with you. When you have a few minutes, look at the cards and practice the words. Do this for several days until you learn the words. If you prefer, use the Houghton Mifflin flash card system on the Internet at http://esl.college.hmco.com/students.

He admitted that he did it.

☐ Linking Concepts

We recognize many things in our daily lives because they are familiar to our senses. Imagine the smell of coffee in the morning, or listening to the radio while driving and recognizing the style of music because of its rhythm or the instruments played. This is what happens when we learn to identify the method of organization used in a reading passage. We become familiar with writing patterns.

When an author writes, he or she uses a particular method to organize the ideas. Usually, more than one pattern is used within a passage, especially depending on its length. Identifying the pattern is important because it allows you to gain a better understanding of what the reading is about. Here are two clues to help you figure out the pattern or method of organization of a reading selection:

1. Identify main ideas and change them into questions.
2. Notice that signal words vary depending on the pattern.

In the previous chapter you worked with a chart that included signal words. The same chart is repeated here with a few additions.

Pattern/function	Signal words
Addition	and, also, too, in addition, moreover, another
Cause/effect	as a result, since, therefore, because, consequently, for that reason, so, affects, causes
Chronology/sequence	all time expressions (including dates), first, second, before, after, then, next, when, a year later, etc.
Classification/listing	A, B, C; 1, 2, 3; • • • •; repetitive phrase patterns
Comparison	both, similarly, in the same way, alike, as well, likewise
Contrast/opposition/ surprise	in contrast, on the other hand, however, nevertheless, instead of, even, but, although, even though
Definition	i.e., that is, this is, ( ), —
Example	e.g., for example, such as, for instance, to demonstrate, are some
Process	first, second, next, then, finally

Remember these words are important to notice when you're reading because they signal supporting details.

Each pattern has special qualities:

A. Addition belongs to all pattern types

B. Cause/Effect patterns show how one thing can influence another. Keep in mind that the cause is what happens first and the effect is what happens second.

C. Chronology/Sequence patterns show the order in which something happens. The order *cannot* be altered.

D. Classification/Listing patterns are simply a list of details whose order can be altered. These details relate to the main idea equally.

E. Comparison/Contrast patterns show the similarities and the differences of two or more things.

F. Definition patterns provide readers with an explanation of terms.

G. Examples belong to all pattern types.

H. Process patterns are similar to Chronology/Sequence but are based on a series of steps.

EXERCISE 20 Identifying patterns of organization

Read the following sentences, and determine which of the following patterns is being used. Write the names of the patterns in the blank spaces. The first one has been done as an example.

Cause/Effect
Comparison/Contrast
Definition
Listing
Sequence

1. _____*Sequence*_____ The spell began to work when the stone arrived in France. It was sold to the French King, Louis. After wearing it once, he became sick and died of smallpox.

2. _____ A superstition is the belief in something that is not based on fact. For example, in English-speaking countries, superstitious people believe that black cats and walking under ladders bring bad luck.

3. _____ She said she did not believe in the diamond's curse. However, she suffered several personal tragedies while she owned the gem.

4. _____ Her son died in a car accident. Her daughter died from an overdose of sleeping pills, and her husband went insane.

5. _____ Evalyn Walsh McLean loved to tell stories. So the stories just kept growing from a very tiny seed of truth.

6. _____ The gem was stolen again at the end of the French Revolution. It appeared in London 38 years later.

7. _____ Monsieur Cartier said that Tavernier stole the gem from a Hindu statue. Because of that, he was cursed and torn apart by wild dogs.

8. _____ A curse is something that causes great evil or harm. For example, the Hope Diamond was said to be cursed because everyone who owned it had a terrible tragedy.

9. _____ Many people believe that the Hope Diamond is cursed, but Jeffrey Post, Curator of the National Gem Collection at the Smithsonian, says that they see the diamond as source of good luck.

10. _____ Louis XIV, Lord Francis Hope, Evalyn Walsh McLean, and Abdul Hamid II are some of the people who owned the Hope Diamond.

⊏⊐ Questions for Review

EXERCISE 21   **Embellishing a story**

Work with a small group of students to do this exercise. Follow these steps:

1. One group member tells a story to the other group members. The story should be simple and true.

2. The group decides how the story can be embellished. You might make things in the story bigger or more exciting. You can also add details that make the story more interesting.

3. Tell your story to another group. The other group must decide which parts of the story are true and which parts are embellishments.

EXERCISE 22 Noticing cultural differences in superstitions

Work as a whole class for this exercise. Follow these steps:

1. Discuss with your classmates any other superstitions they know that come from different cultures.

2. Make a whole-class list of superstitions from different countries. Identify the similarities and differences among the different superstitions.

3. Compare the list with the following common American superstitions or with other American superstitions you may know:

   - Walking under a ladder is bad luck.

   - A black cat is bad luck.

Linking Concepts

EXERCISE 23 Writing in your reading journal

Choose one of the following topics. Write about it in your reading journal.

1. Have you ever embellished a story? Explain why people embellish stories.

2. Describe some superstitions that people believe. How do you think superstitions get started?

3. Why do you think some things are bad luck in some countries but not in others? Give a specific example of something that is bad luck in one country but not in another.

4. The first two reading selections in this chapter have conflicting information about the Hope Diamond. Which reading selection do you think is truer? Explain why you chose the reading selection you did.

5. If you read two things that have different facts about the same topic, how do you decide which one is true?

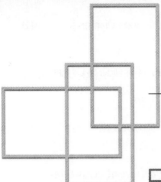

Reading Assignment 3

HOW GEMSTONES ARE FORMED

☐ **Getting Ready to Read**

STRATEGY

Reading Scientific Texts

Reading scientific texts is a little different from reading other texts. Scientific texts have many facts and details. These facts and details are usually very important. So, when you read a scientific text, you need to read a little differently. Here are some helpful suggestions to remember when reading scientific texts:

1. Think about what you already know about the subject.

2. Preview the pictures and diagrams.

3. Read slowly.

EXERCISE 24 **Thinking about what you already know**

Reading Selection 3 is a scientific text from a geology textbook.

a. What is geology?

_____

_____

b. Make a list of some things geologists study.

1. _____

2. _____

3. _____

EXERCISE 25   **Using photographs and diagrams to understand**

Study the photographs and the diagram in this chapter before you read.
Then answer the following questions:

1. What kinds of things do you see in the photographs?

   _____

   _____

2. Have you ever seen photographs like these before? Where?

   _____

   _____

3. What is the diagram about?

   _____

   _____

4. Where are diamonds formed?

   _____

   _____

5. How do diamonds get to Earth's surface?

   _____

   _____

6. Write two questions you have about how diamonds are formed.

   a. _____

   _____

   b. _____

   _____

⬜ Reading the Selection

STRATEGY

Suggestions for Reading Scientific Texts

Read Slowly

Scientific reading is full of facts and details. Read the text slowly to make sure you understand all the details.

Highlight Important Details

One way to slow your reading is to use a highlighting marker or pencil to underline important facts or details as you read. This can also help you review what was important in the reading selection after you read it. As you read Reading Selection 3, underline important details.

Reading Selection 3

HOW GEMSTONES ARE FORMED

Emerald

Topaz

Tourmaline

Beryl

Sapphire

Ruby

Mineral crystal

1 Several minerals lead an exciting life as gemstones. Gemstones are <u>precious</u> or semiprecious minerals that have appealing[1] color, luster,[2] or crystal[3] form. Gemstones can be cut or polished. Some gems, such diamonds and emeralds, are quite <u>rare</u>. Others are quite common. The common ones are crystals of <u>ordinary</u> rock-forming silicates.[4]

1. **ap•peal•ing** (ə-pēl´ĭng) *adj.* Attractive or interesting.
2. **lus•ter** (lŭs´tər) *n.* Soft reflected light.
3. **crys•tal** (krĭs´təl) *n.* A regular geometric shape formed by some substances.
4. **sil•i•cates** (sĭl´ĭ-kĭtz) *n.* A large group of minerals, forming over 90 percent of Earth's crust, that are a combination of silicon and other substances.

2   Minerals form gemstones under conditions that encourage the development of perfect, large crystals. This happens most often in two ways. One way is when molten rock (very hot liquid rock) cools and crystallizes underground. Another way is when preexisting rock is under extraordinary pressure and heat.

3   Molten rock often goes into cracks in surrounding cooler rocks. In the cracks, it produces perfect crystals. If the space is big enough, the molten rock can produce enormous crystals. A single pyroxene crystal excavated[5] in South Dakota was more than 12 meters (40 feet) long and 2 meters (6.5 feet) wide. It weighed more than 8,000 kilograms (8 tons). This process also produces gemstones such as topaz, tourmaline, and beryl.

4   Gemstones may also form when the heat and pressure cause the rock to change. This creates new minerals that are more stable[6] under the new conditions. For example, heat and extreme pressure on rocks that contain aluminum can create rubies and sapphires.

Kimberlite pipe

5   Then there is that rare stone, the diamond. It is transformed from unspectacular carbon into a brilliant[7] crystal by extremely high pressures. Diamonds form at great depths (greater than 150 kilometers, or 90 miles) below the earth's surface. Diamonds most often are found where hot gas has pushed hot liquid rock from deep under the earth to the surface. This liquid rock carries diamonds upward with it. It makes a round structure that looks like a water pipe. These diamond-rich structures are called kimberlite pipes. Kimberlite pipes usually come from deep in the earth. They are named for Kimberley, South Africa. There are kimberlite pipes in Siberia, India, Australia, Brazil, the Northwest Territories of Canada, in southern and central Africa, and the western United States.

6   Only a few kimberlite pipes produce gem-quality diamonds. In southern Africa, only 1 in 200 kimberlite pipes yields[8] enough diamonds to make it worth the high cost of mining them.

5. **ex·ca·vate** (ĕk′skə-vāt′) *tr.v.* To make a hole in something; uncover by digging.
6. **sta·ble** (stā′bəl) *adj.* Not likely to change position or condition.
7. **bril·liant** (brĭl′yənt) *adj.* Full of light; shining brightly.
8. **yield** (yēld) *tr.v.* To give by natural process.

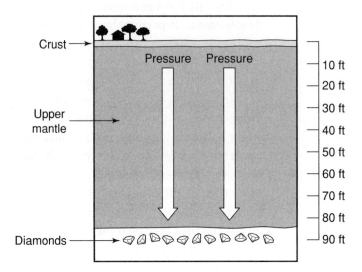

Diamonds form from carbon under pressure of Earth and the heat from the mantle.

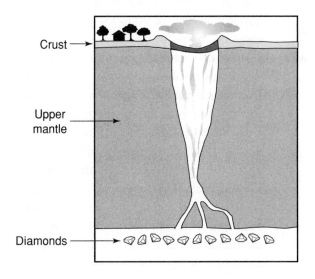

An explosion of gas and molten rock pushes through Earth's surface.

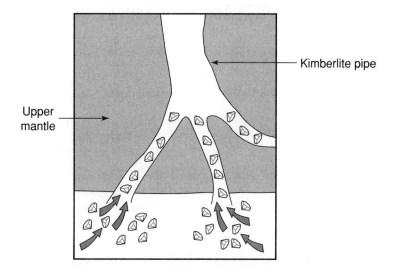

The molten rock quickly carries the diamonds toward Earth's surface.

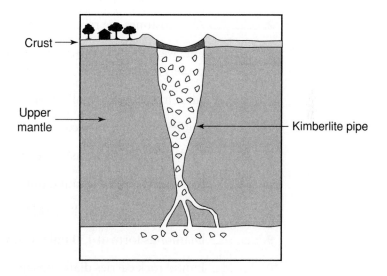

The lava cools, forming a kimberlite pipe.

Source: Adapted from Chernicoff, S. (1999). *Geology: An Introduction to Physical Geology* (2nd ed.). Boston: Houghton Mifflin Company, pp. 58–59.

▭ Assessing Your Learning: How Gemstones Are Formed

Demonstrating Comprehension

EXERCISE 26 **Comparing with a partner**

Look at what kinds of things you underlined in Reading Selection 3. Compare what you underlined with what a partner underlined. Did you choose similar or different things to underline? Discuss with all your classmates how you chose what to underline.

EXERCISE 27 **Understanding the facts**

Tell if each statement is true or false.

1. _____ Gemstones are precious or semiprecious minerals. (¶ 1)

2. _____ All gemstones are rare. (¶ 1)

3. _____ One way gems are formed is when rock cools and crystallizes underground. (¶ 2)

4. _____ All gemstones are small. (¶ 3)

5. _____ Rubies and sapphires contain aluminum. (¶ 4)

6. _____ Carbon is usually transformed into diamonds. (¶ 5)

7. _____ Kimberlite pipes are found only in Africa. (¶ 5)

8. _____ Kimberlite pipes usually yield lots of diamonds. (¶ 6)

9. _____ Diamonds form at 150 miles below the earth's surface. (¶ 5)

10. _____ Liquid rock carries diamonds upward. (¶ 5)

11. _____ When lava heats, a kimberlite pipe is formed. (diagram)

▭ Learning Vocabulary

EXERCISE 28 **Studying academic vocabulary**

These words from Reading Selection 3 are commonly found in academic texts. Study the list below, and learn them by following these guidelines.

1. Number a paper from 1 to 18. Copy these words, leaving spaces for definitions. The paragraph location is provided in parentheses next to the word.
2. Write a definition, synonym, or translation for each word you already know.
3. Compare your list with a partner's. Help each other learn new words.
4. Share your list with your classmates. Your instructor can help you define the words you do not know.

1. precious (¶ 1)	**10.** produces (¶ 3)
2. rare (¶ 1)	**11.** contain (¶ 4)
3. ordinary (¶ 1)	**12.** transform (¶ 5)
4. conditions (¶ 2)	**13.** extremely (¶ 5)
5. extraordinary (¶ 2)	**14.** form (¶ 5)
6. pressure (¶ 2)	**15.** depths (¶ 5)
7. surrounding (¶ 3)	**16.** structure (¶ 5)
8. enormous (¶ 3)	**17.** yield (¶ 6)
9. process (¶ 3)	**18.** mining (¶ 6)

EXERCISE 29 **Definitions from context**

Sometimes the definition of a new word can be found right in the reading text. This makes it easy to learn new words. Define the underlined words in each sentence below by noticing the context.

1. One way is when <u>molten rock</u> (very hot liquid rock) cools and crystallizes underground.

   molten rock = _____

2. This liquid rock carries diamonds upward with it in a round structure that looks like a water pipe. These diamond-rich structures are called <u>kimberlite pipes</u>.

   kimberlite pipes = _____

These words are easy to define because their definitions are in the text. In other cases, you might have to look a little harder to find the definition. For example, can you find the definition of this underlined word?

3. If the space is big enough, the molten rock can produce <u>enormous crystals</u>.

   enormous = _____

4. Look through Reading Selection 3 to find additional definitions in the text.

POWER GRAMMAR

Word Parts

Remember that affixes are word parts that go together to build words. If you know the meanings of the affixes, you can sometimes guess the meanings of words. For example, the affix *pre-* means "before" or "beginning," so a **pre**fix is the beginning of a word; **pre**view means to look at something quickly before you look at it carefully.

EXERCISE 30 Noticing prefixes

Study the list of words and their definitions below. Analyze the meaning of each word part, and then write the meaning of each prefix.

1. semiprecious = half precious   *semi-* = _____

2. unusually = not usually   *un-* = _____

3. preexisting = existing before   *pre-* = _____

4. recombine = combine again   *re-* = _____

5. transformed = changed form   *trans-* = _____

Match each vocabulary word with a word that can follow it in a sentence.

1. semiprecious ____	**a.** condition
2. unusually ____	**b.** gem
3. preexisting ____	**c.** hot
4. transformed ____	**d.** into

⬜ Focusing on Science

EXERCISE 31 **Remembering a process**

In science classes, you are often asked to memorize important facts or processes. Look again at the diagrams that show how a diamond is formed (pp. 156–157). Work with a partner. Cover the words on the page, and tell your partner the process of how a diamond is formed. Your partner should listen to you carefully and add any details you forgot.

EXERCISE 32 **Writing in your reading journal**

Chose one of the following items to include in your reading journal.

1. Draw a diagram for the process of how diamonds are formed. Label the diagram.

Diamond Formation Process
The diamond formation process has four steps. First. . .

2. Write a creative story about your finding a kimberlite pipe with diamonds in it. How did you find it? What did you do when you realized it had diamonds in it? How did the experience change your life?

⬜ Assessing Your Learning at the End of a Chapter

Revisiting Objectives

Return to the first page of this chapter to revisit the chapter objectives. Put a check mark next to the objectives you feel confident about. Review the material in the chapter you need to learn better. When you are ready, take the practice test below. These items reflect the chapter objectives and come from all three reading selections.

🔲 Practicing for a Chapter Test

EXERCISE 33 Reviewing comprehension

Check your comprehension of important material in this chapter by answering the following questions. First, write notes to answer the questions without looking back at the readings. Then, use the readings and exercises to check your answers and revise them. Write your final answers in complete sentences on separate paper.

1. Why is the Hope Diamond important?
2. How did the curse begin?
3. Where does the diamond rest today?
4. Who was Pierre Cartier?
5. What is a superstition?
6. How did the Hope Diamond get its name?
7. Who relates the story in Reading Selection 2?
8. Write the meaning of the following prefixes:
   a. *pre-*   b. *re-*
9. Write the meaning of the following suffixes:
   a. *-less*   b. *-ful*
10. In which pattern of organization are the following words used? *before, after, then, next*
11. Explain two ways in which minerals form gemstones.
12. Write one thing you can do to predict what a reading selection will be about.
13. Why should you read a science text more slowly than some other texts?
14. List the similarities and differences between the Reading Selections 1 and 2.
15. Describe how a graphic organizer can help you take notes.
16. Describe the process for the formation of kimberlite pipes.

▭ Academic Vocabulary Review

Here are some academic vocabulary words that were introduced in this chapter. Confirm the words whose meanings you know. Identify the words that are not yet part of your active vocabulary. Relearn the words you need to.

1. acquire	14. establish	27. ordinary	40. revolution
2. admit	15. extraordinary	28. plenty	41. structure
3. apart	16. extremely	29. powerful	42. supposedly
4. argue	17. final	30. precious	43. surrounding
5. avoid	18. form	31. pressure	44. tiny
6. charm	19. fortune	32. process	45. trade
7. collection	20. impact	33. produces	46. transform
8. conditions	21. management	34. profitable	47. throat
9. contain	22. mining	35. publish	48. unconventional
10. conventional	23. misfortune	36. purchase	49. yield
11. decade	24. misinform	37. rare	
12. depths	25. national	38. reference	
13. enormous	26. ongoing	39. reveal	

EXERCISE 34 **Completing a crossword puzzle**

Complete the crossword puzzle with words from the academic word lists in this chapter. This puzzle will help you review all the academic words you learned in this chapter. Number 7 down and number 25 across have been done for you.

Across

1. not correct information
4. to say something that is true
6. ten years
8. separated
10. front of the neck
12. not usual
15. quickly
16. something that makes a lot of money
18. lots of money; also good luck
19. close in; go around
20. very
23. to produce; to give
25. ordinary; usual
27. to have inside; to hold
28. parts arranged to make a whole thing

Down

2. holy; religious
3. belonging to a nation
5. exchange goods; import and export for example
7. interesting; amusing
9. published source of information
11. assumed to be true
13. bad luck
14. enough; a lot
17. the shape of a thing
21. taking minerals from the earth
22. stay away from
24. deepness
26. disagree

WEB POWER

You will find additional exercises related to the content in this chapter at **elt.heinle.com/collegereading**.

Answer key for the puzzle

	¹M	I	²S	I	N	F	O	R	M	A	T	I	O	³N			
			A							⁴A	D	M	I	⁵T			
	⁶D	E	C	A	D	⁷E			⁸A	P	A	R	T			R	
			R			N		⁹R					I			A	
			E			T		E		¹⁰T	H	R	O	A	T		D
¹¹S			D			E		F				N					E
U					¹²R	A	R	E		¹³M		A		¹⁴P			
P					T		¹⁵R	A	P	I	D	L	Y		E		
¹⁶P	R	O	¹⁷F	I	T	A	B	L	E		S			E			
O			O		I		N		¹⁸F	O	R	T	U	N	E		
¹⁹S	U	R	R	O	U	N	D		C		O			T			
E			M		I		²⁰E	X	T	R	E	M	E	L	Y		
D					N	²²A	V		T		²¹I	N					
L					G	V		U		N							
²³Y	I	E	L	²⁴D		²⁵C	O	N	V	E	N	T	I	O	N	A	²⁶L
				E		I			E		N					R	
				P		D			G		G					G	
	²⁷C	O	N	T	A	I	N								U		
				H				²⁸S	T	R	U	C	T	U	R	E	

Art and Society

ACADEMIC FOCUS: HUMANITIES

Academic Reading Objectives

After completing this chapter,
you should be able to:

✓ Check here as you
master each objective.

1. Improve reading comprehension and gain content knowledge ☐
2. Answer multiple-choice questions ☐
3. Increase your vocabulary by learning words with the same roots ☐
4. Understand the difference between opinions and facts ☐
5. Compare and contrast texts by using a Venn diagram ☐

Humanities Objectives

1. Describe a work of art ☐
2. Explain how sculptures are made ☐
3. Understand the relationship of art and society by studying three works of art ☐
4. Use the Internet and other resources to find out more about a work of art ☐
5. Understand and identify symbolism in art ☐

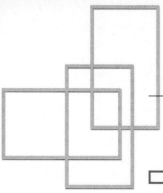

Reading Assignment 1

MICHELANGELO'S *DAVID*

☐ Getting Ready to Read

EXERCISE 1 **Participating in class discussion**

Discuss the following questions with your classmates:

1. Have you ever been to an art museum?
2. What kind of art do you like?
3. Look at the photographs for Reading Selection 1.
   a. Do you recognize the statue in the photograph?
   b. What do you already know about it?
4. a. When was the Renaissance?
   b. What do you know about that time?
5. a. Can you find Florence, Italy, on a map?
   b. What do you know about Florence?
6. a. Who is Michelangelo?
   b. Do you know any other works of art he created?

☐ Reading the Selection

STRATEGY

Comparing Before and After Knowledge

Every time you read, the first thing you should do is ask yourself what you already know about what you are going to read. This will help you better remember what you read.

EXERCISE 2 Comparing before and after knowledge

Before you read this selection, write down all the information you already know about the topic. You could use the questions in the "Getting Ready to Read" section as a guide.

Michelangelo's *David*	
What I already know	**What I learned**

After you read Reading Selection 1, be prepared to complete the "What I Learned" part of your chart.

Reading Selection 1

MICHELANGELO'S *DAVID*

The Rejection of Michelangelo's *David*

1   Since early people drew on cave walls, art has been important to society. Art tells us about the people who live in a society. It can tell what is important for the people. Art can help us understand how people live. However, not all works of art are welcomed by a society right away. An example of this is Michelangelo's statue[1] *David*. It is one of the most recognized pieces of art. It is considered a masterpiece[2] of Renaissance[3] art. But not everyone liked it when it was first displayed. You may be surprised to know that many well-known works of art were not accepted when the public first saw them.

2   Why was the *David* so unpopular? A group of people called Opera del Duomo ("Works of the Cathedral") in Florence, Italy, paid Michelangelo to create the statue. The Opera del Duomo was a group of people that made sure the Cathedral[4] was properly maintained. It also looked after the works of art. The group wanted a statue to be prominently displayed in the plaza[5] outside of the Cathedral. The statue was important because the plaza was the main public meeting place for the people of Florence.

3   The Opera del Duomo told Michelangelo to make a statue of David. Choosing David was a political statement. David represented the victory of a little person over the powerful giant Goliath. For the people of Florence, it symbolized their city's freedom. Before this, Florence had been ruled by outsiders. So, the people of Florence thought they were like David. They considered the outsiders to be like Goliath. Everyone in Florence knew why David was the subject of the statue. Florence was telling the world that a small city could free itself from more powerful outsiders.

---

1. **stat•ue** (stăch´o͞o) *n.* A form or likeness made of stone, metal, clay, or wood.
2. **mas•ter•piece** (măs´tər-pēs´) *n.* An outstanding work.
3. **Ren•ais•sance** (rĕn´ĭ-säns´) *n.* The revival of classical art, literature, architecture, and learning in Europe from the fourteenth through the sixteenth century.
4. **ca•the•dral** (kə-thē´drəl) *n.* The principal church of a bishop's diocese.
5. **pla•za** (plä´zə) *n.* A public square of similar open area in a town or city.

4   Michelangelo started working on the sculpture in 1501. It was not an easy job. The marble[6] block was sixteen feet high. It had been cut from the mountain forty years earlier. Other famous sculptors[7] like Leonardo da Vinci thought about carving this huge piece of marble. However, the marble had many cracks in it. Whoever carved it would have to be very careful. The cracks could ruin the whole statue. Many artists had made sculptures of David. Michelangelo's *David* was different. He made David a larger-than-life hero. But it was a hero with human qualities. The statue shows David getting ready to fight the giant. He is human because his face has a frown of concentration.

5   It took Michelangelo three years to complete the statue. It took forty men four days to move the statue six hundred yards to the plaza. It took another twenty days to raise it on to the platform. During this time, many people protested against[8] the statue. They threw rocks at the statue. Guards were hired to prevent people from damaging it. Why did they protest? Some people supported the outsiders. They thought that the statue was an insult. Other people complained because the statue had no clothes. Before it was officially revealed to the public, *David* was covered with a skirt of copper leaves. Today, the skirt has been removed. The people of Florence did not protest long. Within ten years, Michelangelo's statue of David was the pride of Florence. It is seen as a cultural symbol of the city.

6   It seems surprising that the *David* had such a controversial beginning. It is one of the most famous and admired statues. Today we do not think of the *David* as a political statement. We only consider it as a fine work of art. The *David* is an example of how society influences art and of how art influences society. It also shows how public attitudes about art can change over time.

Source: Information compiled by author from Preble, D., & Preble S. (1999). *Artforms* (6th ed.). Addison-Wesley, pp. 298–299 and Sayre, H. (2003). *A World of Art* (4th ed.). Columbus, OH: Prentice-Hall, pp. 68–69.

---

6. **mar·ble** (mär´bəl) *n.* A type of hard stone used for buildings, sculpture, and monuments.
7. **sculp·tor** (skŭlp´tər) *n.* An artist who makes sculptures.
8. **pro·test a·gainst** (prō´tĕst´ ə-gĕnst´) *v.* To express strong objections to something in a formal statement or a public demonstration.

⬜ Assessing Your Learning: Michelangelo's *David*

Demonstrating Comprehension

STRATEGY

Multiple Choice

One type of reading comprehension exercise that is used frequently on tests is multiple choice. Sometimes these questions can be tricky. Sometimes there is more than one correct answer. You must be careful when reading multiple-choice questions. It is important to read all the answers before you choose one. Many times, one of the choices will be "all of the above." This phrase means that all the different choices are correct. If you do not read all the answers, you might think the first answer is the correct choice and not consider the other answers.

For example, look at question 1 in Exercise 3.
Reading Selection 1 says:

> Art tells us about the people who live in a society. It can tell what is important for the people. Art can help us understand how people live.

According to the reading selection, then, answers a, b, and c are all correct. In this case, you should mark answer "d. all of the above."

EXERCISE 3 Reading multiple-choice questions carefully

As you answer the rest of the questions, make sure you read all the choices carefully. Choose the best completion.

1. From works of art we can learn
   a. about the people who live in a society.
   b. how people live.
   c. what is important for people.
   d. all of the above

2. Michelangelo's *David*
   a. is a statue.
   b. is a painting.
   c. has always been loved.
   d. all of the above

3. The Opera del Duomo
   a. was a group of opera singers.
   b. took care of the Cathedral.
   c. was a group of people who lived in the Cathedral.
   d. all of the above

4. The idea to make a statue of David
   a. was the idea of the Opera del Duomo.
   b. was a political statement.
   c. represented the victory of Florence over outsiders.
   d. all of the above

5. The marble from which Michelangelo made the statue
   a. was similar to the marble Leonardo da Vinci had carved.
   b. had many cracks in it.
   c. came from Florence.
   d. all of the above

6. We can guess that the statue is heavy because
   a. it is made of marble.
   b. it took four days to move it to the plaza.
   c. it took twenty days to put it on the platform.
   d. all of the above

EXERCISE 4   **Answering comprehension questions**

Write the answers to the following questions:

1. What are the two reasons not everybody liked the statue of David when it was first completed?
2. Why was the *David* displayed in the plaza?
3. What does the *David* symbolize?
4. The marble block had been cut from the mountain forty years earlier. Why did it take so long for someone to carve something from the block?
5. The *David* represented both a hero and a human. Explain why this is true.
6. Describe the people's reaction to the statue when it was first displayed.

▭ Learning Vocabulary

EXERCISE 5 Studying academic vocabulary

These words from Reading Selection 1 are commonly found in academic texts. Study the list of words below, and then learn them by following these guidelines:

1. Number a paper from 1 to 10. Copy these words, leaving spaces for definitions. The paragraph location is provided in parentheses next to the word.
2. Write a definition, synonym, or translation for each word you already know.
3. Compare your list with a partner's. Help each other learn new words.
4. Share your list with your classmates. Your instructor can help you define the words you do not know.

1. displayed (¶ 1)   5. job (¶ 4)   9. symbol (¶ 5)
2. create (¶ 2)   6. revealed (¶ 5) 10. controversial (¶ 6)
3. maintained (¶ 2)   7. removed (¶ 5)   11. attitudes (¶ 6)
4. symbolized (¶ 2)   8. cultural (¶ 5)

POWER GRAMMAR

Noticing Collocations

Many times, words in English are grouped together in phrases called collocations. You can improve your vocabulary by remembering not only words but also other words commonly found before the word.

EXERCISE 6 Working with collocation

The word boxes on the next page show some academic words and some other words that are usually put together with them. Study the words, and then learn them by following these guidelines:

1. Say the words out loud together in phrases. For example, say "clearly displayed," "proudly displayed," "prominently displayed."

2. Look up the dictionary meaning of any words you do not know.
3. Work with a partner. Write each word below on a note card. Write each word from the left column in black ink. Write the academic words from the right column in red ink. Mix up the note cards. Try to match the academic words with the correct collocation.

clearly proudly prominently		displayed
properly well poorly		maintained
fine good professional difficult hard	easy important big small	job
completely temporarily quickly	easily painlessly	removed
clear powerful cultural	traditional political	symbol
extremely highly very politically		controversial
positive friendly bad	critical negative public	attitude

POWER GRAMMAR

Noticing How Words Are Used

The same word can have more than one meaning. Many words in English have more than one definition. Which definition is correct also depends on the part of speech.

EXERCISE **7**   **Selecting definitions**

Each word below has more than one meaning. Find each word in Reading Selection 1. Then select the correct definition of the word as it is used in the reading selection.

1. public (¶ 1)

   a. freely available   **b.** community

2. recognize (¶ 1)

   a. to be familiar with   **b.** acknowledge

3. maintain (¶ 2)

   a. take care of   **b.** argue for something

4. job (¶ 4)

   a. profession   **b.** task

5. block (¶ 4)

   a. stop   **b.** a large piece

6. raise (¶ 5)

   a. lift up   **b.** improve

7. skirt (¶ 5)

   a. avoid   **b.** a piece of clothing

▢ **Focusing on Art**

Read this additional information about sculpture carving and Michelangelo in order to add to your knowledge about art.

HOW SCULPTURES ARE MADE

Michelangelo's *David* is an example of a sculpture that is carved. Carving is the most difficult kind of sculpture because there is no opportunity to correct errors. Before beginning to cut, an artist must visualize all angles of the finished form. Artists usually carve sculptures out of stone or wood. Different kinds of stone cause different problems for the artist. Three common types of stone are sandstone, marble, and granite. Sandstone is course. It is difficult to carve it exactly. Marble is soft to carve, but can have cracks like the block that Michelangelo used to carve the *David* from. The artist must study the block of stone very well first in order to find the weaknesses. Granite is a very hard stone. It takes strength to carve in granite. After they have finished carving the figure, the artists must file and polish the stone until it shines. Michelangelo believed that his job was to release the figure from the block of marble.

Source: Information complied by author from Sayre, H. *A. World of Art*, 4th ed. (2003), Prentice Hall, pp. 500–503: PBS website, www.pbs.org/treasureoftheworld/guernica/gmain.html

Michelangelo Buonarroti

BIOGRAPHY OF MICHELANGELO

Michelangelo Buonarroti was born in a small village near Florence. When he was young, he learned to be a painter and sculptor. Even his early paintings and sculptures showed a unique personal style. When he was a young man, political problems in Florence made it necessary for him to go to Rome, Italy, where he created several sculptures including the famous *Pieta*. Shortly after that he started to work on the "David." In 1508 the Pope called him to Rome. The Pope wanted Michelangelo to paint the ceiling of one of his churches. For four years he painted what is known today as one of the most beautiful works of art in the world, the ceiling of the Sistine Chapel. Because of the political problems of his lifetime, Michelangelo went back and forth between Florence and Rome. His mark is left on both cities with some of the greatest works of Renaissance art. These include sculptures like the Tomb of Julius II and the Medici Tombs and the painting of the "Last Judgment." Michelangelo was also an architect and a poet. He died at the age of 70.

Source: Information complied by author from Sayre, H. *A. World of Art*, 4th ed. (2003), Prentice Hall, pp. 500–503: PBS website, www.pbs.org/treasureoftheworld/guernica/gmain.html

🔲 Questions for Review

EXERCISE 8 **Answering questions in a small group**

*Make a group of three or four students. With your group members, discuss
the following questions. Share your answers with your other classmates.*

1. Do you agree with the statement "Society influences art and art
   influences society"? Explain why you agree or disagree.
2. For the people of Florence, the *David* was a symbol of freedom.
   What would be a symbol of freedom today? With your group
   members, make a list of things that are symbols of freedom for you.
3. Study the photographs of the *David* in Reading Selection 1. Imagine
   someone who had never seen a photograph of Michelangelo's
   David. With your group, write a description of the statue that will
   help that person visualize it accurately.
4. Explain the different types of stone used by artists and the difficulty
   artists face when working with each one.
5. What are some other works Michelangelo created?

🔲 Linking Concepts

EXERCISE 9 **Doing research**

*The information in Reading Selection 1 does not explain everything about
Michelangelo's David. Use the Internet or reference books to find more
information. Share the information you find with your classmates. Here are
some possible topics. Your instructor may suggest more.*

- The Renaissance
- Michelangelo
- Other Statues of *David*
- Other statues by Michelangelo
- Paintings by Michelangelo
- Florence
- Symbolism in art
- Current location and condition of the *David*

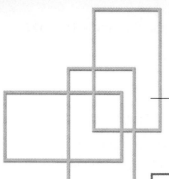

Reading Assignment 2

MAYA LIN'S VIETNAM MEMORIAL

▭ Getting Ready to Read

EXERCISE **10** **Participating in class discussion**

Discuss the following questions with your classmates:

1. What are some ways people remember those who die in wars?
2. What do you know about the Vietnam War?
3. Have you ever heard of the Vietnam Veterans Memorial? What do you know about it?

Reading Selection 2

MAYA LIN'S VIETNAM MEMORIAL

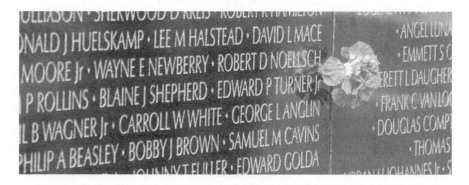

1   Another example of the <u>public</u> first <u>rejecting</u> and then coming to understand and accept a work of art is Maya Lin's Vietnam memorial.[1] A group of war veterans had the idea to create a monument. They set up a contest for the <u>design</u> of a monument. Lin's design was <u>selected</u> from a group of more than 1,400 entries. Lin was twenty-two years old when she won the contest. She had just graduated from Yale University, where she studied architecture.[2]

1. **Vi·et·nam** (vē-ĕt'näm') *n.* A country in Southeast Asia.
2. **ar·chi·tec·ture** (är'kĭ-tĕk'chər) *n.* The art and occupation of designing and directing the construction of buildings and other large structures.

2   In Washington, most war monuments[3] are statues of famous people or events from a war. An example of this is the Marine Corps World War II monument near Washington. The monument illustrates a scene from a famous battle. It shows the planting of the American flag on a hill at Iwo Jima. At first, the Vietnam memorial did not have any statues. It's design was very different from the other monuments in other ways. Most of the other Washington monuments rise above the ground level; Maya Lin designed her memorial to actually go below ground level.

3   The *Vietnam Veterans Memorial* now consists of three parts: the Wall, the Three Servicemen Statue and Flagpole, and the Vietnam Women's Memorial. Lin's design was for the Wall, which represents the war in a more abstract way. It goes down below ground in a giant V. It is more than two hundred feet long on each side. The Wall is covered with the names of the more than 58,000 American men and women who died in the war. Their names, cut into the Wall, are listed in the order in which they died. The Wall is made of polished black granite.[4] If you stand in front of it, the granite reflects your own image back at you. It seems to say that your life is what these people fought for. As you walk down to the middle of the V, the height of the Wall and the number of names in each panel increases. Now you are well below ground level, and the Wall and names tower above you. This shows that in the middle of the war more and more people were killed.

4   The non-traditional design of the initial memorial upset many people. They thought it was an insult to those who died in the war. Some called it a "black gash[5] of shame." Others called it a "giant tombstone."[6] They wanted a more traditional monument. They wanted statues of people. They wanted something grand like the other monuments in Washington. Some people were also upset that the winning design belonged to an Asian-American[7] woman. Some wanted to throw out the design and start the contest over again.

3. **mon•u•ment** (mŏn´yə-mənt) *n.* A structure such as a tower or statue, built to honor a person, a group, or an event.
4. **gran•ite** (grăn´ĭt) *n.* A common coarse-grained, hard rock used in buildings and monuments.
5. **gash** (găsh) *n.* A long deep cut or wound.
6. **tomb•stone** (to̅o̅m´sto̅n´) *n.* A monument marking a grave or tomb.
7. **A•sian A•mer•i•can** (ā´zhen ə-mer´ĭ-kən) *n.* An american of Asian descent who grows up in the United States.

Even government officials were upset. The U.S. Secretary of the Interior[8] would not issue a building permit for the memorial.

5   It looked like there would not be a memorial at all. Supporters and opponents of Lin's design met to find a compromise.[9] They decided to add a statue that represented the soldiers who fought during the war. This would make a more traditional memorial. The compromise made opponents of Lin's design happy. Today, a statue of three male soldiers, and a statue of women veterans of the Vietnam War, stand near the Wall. Together, these three components make up what is now called the Vietnam Veterans Memorial.

6   When the Wall monument was opened, its beauty surprised people. It has a powerful effect on people. Today, the Vietnam Veterans Memorial is the most visited monument in Washington. The wall of the memorial is seen as a strong symbol. It helps Americans remember the people who died during the war. It is also seen as a way for the American people to heal the injuries caused by the war. It is so admired by Americans that they affectionately[10] call the memorial "The Wall."

7   Maya Lin describes how she got the idea for the memorial:
I thought about what death is; what a loss is. A sharp pain that lessens with time, but can never quite heal over. A scar.[11] The idea occurred to me there on the site. Take a knife and cut open the earth, and with time the grass would heal it. As if you cut open the rock and polished it.

The Vietnam Veterans Memorial is another example of how art influences society and society influences art.

Source: Source: Information compiled by author from Sayre, H. (2003). *A World of Art* (4th ed.). Columbus, OH: Prentice-Hall, pp. 64–65 and Campbell, R. (1983, May). An Emotive Place Apart, *AIA Journal*, p. 151.

8. **Sec•re•tar•y of the In•te•ri•or** (sĕk´rĭ-tĕr´ē ŭv thē ĭn-tîr´ē-ər) *n.* One of the officials who advises the president of the Unites. The Secretary of the Interior is in charge of the use of public lands and natural resources.
9. **com•pro•mise** (kŏm´prə-mīz´) *n.* A settlement of an argument in which each side gives up some of what it wants.
10. **af•fec•tion•ate•ly** (ə-fĕk´shə-nĭt-lē) *adv.* With a fond and tender feeling toward someone or something.
11. **scar** (skär) *n.* A mark left on the skin after a wound or injury has healed.

⬜ Assessing Your Learning: Maya Lin's Vietnam Memorial

Demonstrating Comprehension

EXERCISE 11 Distinguishing true or false statements

Read the following statements. If the statement is true, write T. If the statement is false, write F and rewrite the statement to make it true. The first one has been done for you as an example.

1. ___f___ Maya Lin was a ~~well-known~~ ^young^ artist when she won the contest.

2. _____ The Marine Corps World War II monument is typical of most monuments in the Washington area.

3. _____ The Wall of the Vietnam Veterans Memorial is different because it rises above the ground.

4. _____ The names are listed on the Wall in alphabetical order.

5. _____ The Wall reflects what is in front of it.

6. _____ Some people thought the design was insulting.

7. _____ The design was non-traditional.

8. _____ Government officials supported the design.

9. _____ The supporters and opponents were not able to make a compromise.

10. _____ People changed their minds about the monument after it opened.

11. _____ For Maya Lin, making a cut into the earth was a symbol of the pain of death.

Abstract Ideas

Maya Lin chose to represent the Vietnam War in an abstract way. Instead of making a specific representation of an event or a person from the war, she chose to give a general idea of the whole war. The gentle slope of the Wall shows how the war began slowly. The increasing number of names represents how the war got worse. Lin wants us to see how the war is like a scar that never completely heals. She also represents this in an abstract way by making a cut into the earth. Abstract means something that is based on a general idea rather than a specific example or real event.

EXERCISE 12 Understanding abstract ideas

Here are some examples of abstract ideas. Work with a partner. Explain how an artist might represent these abstract ideas.

Beauty
Freedom
Pain
Happiness

▭ Learning Vocabulary

EXERCISE 13 Studying academic vocabulary

These words from Reading Selection 2 are commonly found in academic texts. Study the list of words below, and then learn them by following these guidelines:

1. Number a paper from 1 to 10. Copy these words, leaving spaces for definitions. The paragraph location is provided in parentheses next to each word.
2. Write a definition, synonym, or translation for each word you already know.
3. Compare your list with a partner's. Help each other learn new words.
4. Share your list with your classmates. Your instructor can help you define the words you do not know.

1. public (¶ 1)	**6.** illustrates (¶ 2)	**11.** issue (¶ 4)
2. rejecting (¶ 1)	**7.** abstract (¶ 3)	**12.** symbol (¶ 6)
3. create (¶ 1)	**8.** image (¶ 3)	**13.** injuries (¶ 6)
4. design (¶ 1)	**9.** panel (¶ 3)	**14.** occurred (¶ 7)
5. selected (¶ 1)	**10.** non-traditional (¶ 4)	**15.** site (¶ 7)

POWER GRAMMAR

Word Forms

Some words have similar roots but are used in different forms. For example, here are three different forms of the word *compete*:

She is a **competitive** person.
She entered the art **competition**.
She likes to **compete**.

EXERCISE **14** **Studying word families**

Complete the chart by writing the base word and its meaning. The first one has been done for you as an example.

Noun	Verb	Adjective	Adverb	Base Word	Meaning
1. competition competitor competitiveness	compete	competitive	competitively	compete	try to win or be successful
2. rejection	reject	rejected			
3. abstraction		abstract	abstractly		
4. design designer	design				
5. nation	nationalize	national	nationally		
6. reflection	reflect	reflecting			
7. memorial	memorialize	memorial			
8. tradition		traditional	traditionally		
9. opponent opposition	oppose	opposing opposite			
10. supporter	support	supporting			
11. symbol	symbolize	symbolic	symbolically		
12. admiration	admire	admiring			
13. affection		affectionate	affectionately		

EXERCISE 15 **Using the correct form**

Complete the following sentences with the correct word form from the chart above. The first one has been done for you as an example.

1. Maya Lin is a tough *competitor* _____.

2. At first, many people wanted to _____ her design for the Vietnam memorial.

3. Maya Lin represents the war _____.

4. Her _____ won the contest.

5. Now the Wall of the Vietnam Veterans Memorial is an object of _____ pride.

6. You can see your _____ in the polished black granite.

7. One way to remember people who have died is to _____ them.

8. Building war monuments is a _____ in the United States.

9. The two sides had _____ viewpoints.

10. Now most Americans _____ the Vietnam Memorial.

11. The Wall _____ the men and women who died in the war.

12. Many Americans _____ the Vietnam Veterans Memorial every year.

13. Americans have great _____ for the Vietnam Veterans Memorial.

EXERCISE 16   Finding and writing opposites

One way to remember new words is to relate them to their opposites. In Reading Selection 2, find the opposite of each of the following words or phrases. Write the opposite on the line.

1. rejecting (¶ 1)   *coming to understand*

2. goes below (¶ 2)   _____

3. non-traditional (¶ 4)   _____

4. supporters (¶ 5)   _____

▭ Questions for Review

EXERCISE 17   Participating in group work

Work with a group of three or four other students. Answer the following questions:

1. Maya Lin says she got her idea for the memorial by thinking about death and the loss of someone. What are some other ways you could symbolize death and/or loss?

2. Many people changed their minds about the Wall memorial after it was opened. Why do you think they changed their minds?

3. Lin's original idea about the memorial was changed by adding the statues of three male soldiers and of women who were in the war. Do you think these were a good compromise or not? Explain.

4. Compare the Reading Selections 1 and 2. How are the stories of the *David* and the Wall of the Vietnam Veterans Memorial similar? How are they different? How are the two artworks similar? How are they different? With your group, make a large copy of the Venn diagram below. Put the things that are similar in the middle section.

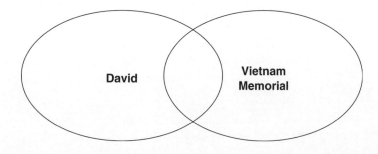

▭ Linking Concepts

EXERCISE **18** **Writing in your reading journal**

Respond to one or more of the following in your journal:

1. Write your personal answer to one of the questions from Exercise 17.

2. Write a comparison and/or contrast composition about the *David* and the Wall of the Vietnam Veterans Memorial by using the Venn diagram your group created.

3. In what ways do both pieces of art represent freedom?

4. Study the illustrations of the Vietnam Veterans Memorial in Reading Selection 2. Imagine someone who had never seen a photograph of Maya Lin's Wall at the Vietnam Veterans Memorial. Write a description of the Wall that will help the person visualize it accurately.

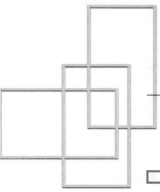

Reading Assignment 3

PABLO PICASSO'S *GUERNICA*

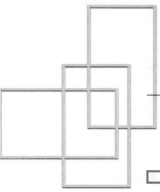

Getting Ready to Read

EXERCISE 19 Participating in class discussion

Discuss the following questions with your classmates:

1. Who is Pablo Picasso?
2. Do you know any works of art that he created?
3. Look at the illustration of the painting *Guernica* in this text. Have you ever seen the painting before?
4. What is your first impression of the painting?
5. What do you think it means?

Pablo Picasso

▭ **Reading the Selection**

EXERCISE 20 **Finding and describing symbols**

In Reading Selection 3, paragraph 3 describes the symbols in the painting Guernica. *As you read, look at the painting to find the symbols described in the reading selection. Beside the illustration in your book, write what the different parts of the painting illustrate.* The bull represents Spain.

Reading Selection 3

PABLO PICASSO'S *GUERNICA*

1 The mural[1] *Guernica* is one of the most powerful modern paintings. It is an important antiwar[2] statement. Pablo Picasso painted the mural for the 1937 World's Fair. He is the 20th century's most well known artist.

2 For three months, Picasso tried to find an idea for the mural. Picasso was a native of Spain. The politics of his country worried him. Spain was in the middle of a <u>civil</u> war. Still, Picasso did not think that art and politics go together. He stayed away from political <u>themes</u> in his art. Still, he could not <u>ignore</u> the events of April 27th, 1937. Spanish and German fascists attacked a little town in northern Spain. Bombs dropped on Guernica for over three

Picasso's *Guernica*

1. **mu·ral** (myŏŏr´əl) *n.* A large painting or decoration created directly on a wall or ceiling.
2. **an·ti·war** (ăn´tī-wôr´) *adj.* Opposing war.

hours. People, including women and children, were killed as they ran from the buildings. The small town burned for three days. 1,600 people were killed or wounded.

3   The photographs of the attack shocked Picasso. He created the huge mural to show his shock. Picasso did not represent the horror of Guernica realistically. In fact, *Guernica* is considered one of the greatest paintings of Surrealism.[3] For Surrealists symbols and dreams are important. Different parts of the mural have symbolic meaning. The bull represents Spain. The dead people lying across the ground represent the suffering of war. Suffering is also represented in the mother and child. The contrast between the light bulb and the lantern are also important. They represent the old and new ways of seeing things. The whole mural represents Picasso's dream of the terror of war.

4   Picasso's *Guernica* was a main attraction at the World's Fair. However, the first reaction to the painting was not totally positive. A German critic called *Guernica* a mural that "any four-year-old could have painted."

5   Today, this painting is considered an important criticism[4] of war. A copy of the painting hangs in the United Nations.[5] This is to remind the members of the United Nations of the horror of war.

6   After the World's Fair, *Guernica* was displayed at different locations in Europe and the Americas. It was usually in New York at the Museum of Modern Art but was also displayed in several countries around the world. However, Picasso would not let it be displayed in Spain. Picasso always wanted the mural to be owned by the Spanish people. However, he refused to allow it to travel to Spain until Spain had a democratic[6] government. In 1985, *Guernica* finally returned to Spain. Spaniards can now see it at the Reina Sophia museum in Madrid, Spain.

Source: Information compiled by author from Sayre, H. (2003). *A World of Art* (4th ed.). Columbus, OH: Prentice Hall, pp. 500–503 and PBS website www.pbs.org/treasuresoftheworld/guernica/gmain.html

---

3. **sur•re•al•ism** (sə-rē´ə-lĭz´əm) *n.* A twentieth-century literary and artistic movement attempting to show dreams and other products of the unconscious mind.
4. **crit•i•cism** (krĭt´ĭ-sĭz´əm) *n.* The art or profession of forming and expressing judgments, especially about literary or artistic works.
5. **U•nit•ed Na•tions** (yōō-nī´tĭd nā´shənz) *n.* An international organization made up of representatives from most of the countries of the world. It works to solve the political problems in the world.
6. **dem•o•crat•ic** (dĕm´ə-krăt´ĭk) *adj.* Of or for people in general.

Master Student Tip

▼ A fact is generally accepted reality, something that informed people agree about. An opinion, on the other hand, is a belief or a conclusion that not everyone agrees about. For example:

The sun rises in the east. (This is a fact. The sun always comes up in the east, moves across the sky, and sets in the west.)
This is the most beautiful sunrise. (This is an opinion. Some people may believe that this sunrise is the most beautiful sunrise, but others may disagree.)

In these two examples, it is easy to tell fact from opinion. Sometimes it is more difficult.

☐ Assessing Your Learning: Pablo Picasso's *Guernica*

Demonstrating Comprehension

EXERCISE 21   **Distinguishing fact from opinion**

Read each of the following statements, which come from Reading Selection 3. Write F if the statement is a fact. Write O if the statement is an opinion. Write the reason you believe it is a fact or an opinion. The paragraph where the sentence is found is in parentheses at the end of the sentence. The first one has been done for you as an example.

1. ___O___ The mural *Guernica* is one of the most powerful modern paintings. (¶ 1)

   Some people might think it is powerful, but other people might think another modern painting is more powerful.

2. _____ He is the 20th century's most well known artist. (¶ 1)

3. _____ Spain was in the middle of a civil war. (¶ 2)

4. _____ 1,600 people were killed or wounded. (¶ 2)

5. _____ In fact, *Guernica* is considered one of the greatest paintings of Surrealism. (¶ 3)

6. _____ . . . *Guernica* [is] a mural that "any four-year-old could have painted." (¶ 4)

7. _____ Today, this painting is considered an important criticism of war. (¶ 5)

8. _____ A copy of the painting hangs in the United Nations. (¶ 5)

9. _____ After the World's Fair, *Guernica* was displayed at different locations . . . (¶ 6)

10. _____ Spaniards can now see it at the Reina Sophia museum in Madrid, Spain. (¶ 6)

☐ Learning Vocabulary

EXERCISE 22   **Studying academic vocabulary**

These words from Reading Selection 3 are commonly found in academic texts. Study the list of words below, and then learn them by following these guidelines:

1. Number a paper from 1 to 10. Copy these words, leaving spaces for definitions. The paragraph location is provided in parentheses next to each word.
2. Write a definition, synonym, or translation for each word you already know.
3. Compare your list with a partner's. Help each other learn new words.
4. Share your list with your classmates. Your instructor can help you define the words you do not know.

1. civil (¶ 2)	**6.** contrast (¶ 3)
2. themes (¶ 2)	**7.** reaction (¶ 4)
3. ignore (¶ 2)	**8.** positive (¶ 4)
4. created (¶ 3)	**9.** displayed (¶ 6)
5. symbolic (¶ 3)	**10.** locations (¶ 6)

Match each vocabulary word with the words that can follow it in a sentence.

1. civil _____	**a.** the events
2. ignore _____	**b.** meaning
3. created _____	**c.** the huge mural
4. symbolic _____	**d.** war
5. contrast _____	**e.** in Europe
6. reaction _____	**f.** three works of art
7. location _____	**g.** to

EXERCISE 23   **Completing a word puzzle**

Using the clues below, complete the word puzzle with academic words.

		1			P						
		2			A						
		3			B						
	4				L						
		5			O						
		6			P						
		7			I						
			8		C						
			9		A						
10					S						
11					S						
				12	O						

1. not permanent
2. made, produced
3. representing something else
4. relating to the people who live in a country
5. do not pay attention to something
6. put on view, show
7. not negative
8. places
9. response; what you feel because of something you have seen
10. pictures; photos
11. topics, ideas
12. difference

▭ Focusing on Art

Read this additional information about abstract art to add to your knowledge about art.

Symbolism

Abstract art is a painting or sculpture that represents objects in a stylized or simplified way. In an abstract painting, you will be able to recognize the image, but it will not look realistic. Picasso's *Guernica* is an abstract painting. He chose to represent the bull, the horse, and the people injured in war not how they really look, but in a stylized and simplified way. You learned in Reading Selection 3 that each of these parts is a symbol. It has symbolic meaning. Artists often use symbols in their work.

Below is a painting by Marc Chagall. The painting is titled *Paris through the Window*. It was painted in 1913. Work with a group of three or four other students. Study the painting carefully. Discuss the meaning of the different parts of the painting with your group.

What do you think the different parts symbolize?

Marc Chagall's *Paris through the Window*

▭ Questions for Review

EXERCISE 24 **Answering questions in a small group**

Work with a group of three or four other students. Answer the following questions:

1. Have you ever visited an art museum? Visit a local art museum. (You might do this with your class.) See if you can find symbols in the different artworks. If you cannot go to a museum, search museum Internet sites. Check our website at http://esl.college.hmco.com/students for suggested Internet sites to visit.

2. To understand some symbols, you must know something about the religion or culture of the artist. Find a work of art from a religion or culture you know well, and explain the symbols to your group members. You can find pictures in books or on the Internet. You might show your group an example of a Buddha or other religious symbol or folk art from your native country.

3. Do you think artists should be involved in politics? Do you think Picasso's *Guernica* is an effective antiwar statement? Explain.

▭ Linking Concepts

EXERCISE 25 **Writing in your reading journal**

Respond to one or more of the following in your journal:

1. Write a description of your visit to the museum.

2. Compare and contrast all three works of art you studied in this chapter.

3. Write your personal response to these questions:

    a. Do you think artists should be involved in politics? Why/why not?

    b. Do you think Picasso's *Guernica* is an effective antiwar statement? Why/why not?

☐ Assessing Your Learning at the End of a Chapter

Revisiting Objectives

Return to the first page of this chapter to revisit the chapter objectives. Put a check mark next to the objectives you feel confident about. Review the material in the chapter you need to learn better. When you are ready, take the practice test in Exercise 26. These items reflect the chapter objectives and come from all three reading selections.

☐ Practicing for a Chapter Test

EXERCISE 26   **Reviewing comprehension**

Check your comprehension of important material in this chapter by answering the following questions. First, write notes to answer the questions without looking back at the readings. Then, use the readings and exercises to check your answers and revise them. Write your final answers in complete sentences on separate paper.

1. What should you do when answering multiple-choice questions? Why should you do this?
2. In the chart, match the academic words with the words that are commonly found before them. Each academic word will have more than one matching word.

First words	Next words (academic words)
1. clearly 2. completely 3. critical 4. difficult 5. highly 6. painlessly 7. positive 8. powerful 9. professional 10. properly 11. proudly 12. traditional 13. very	_____ controversial _____ displayed _____ job _____ maintained _____ removed _____ symbol _____ attitude

3. Explain the difference between a fact and an opinion. Explain how you recognize it in a text.

4. Choose the correct form of the word to complete each sentences:

   A. An art _____ decided who would create the Vietnam Memorial.
   a. competitive   **b.** competition   **c.** competitively

   B. At first, no one accepted it. It was a _____ piece of art.
   a. rejection   **b.** reject   **c.** rejected

   C. Freedom is an _____ idea.
   a. abstraction   **b.** abstract   **c.** abstractly

   D. The "Wall" _____ your image.
   a. reflection   **b.** reflects   **c.** reflecting

   E. The Vietnam Memorial is not _____.
   a. tradition   **b.** traditional   **c.** traditionally

   F. Someone who is not a supporter is an _____.
   a. opponent   **b.** oppose   **c.** opposing

   G. A _____ of the United States is the Statue of Liberty.
   a. symbol   **b.** symbolize   **c.** symbolic

5. Compare one of the other artworks you learned about in this chapter with Picasso's *Guernica*. Make a Venn diagram. (See example in this chapter).

6. Study the illustrations of Picasso's *Guernica* in Reading Selection 3. Imagine someone who had never seen a photograph of *Guernica*. With your group, write a description of the mural that will help the person visualize it accurately.

7. Explain this statement: "Society influences art and art influences society." Use examples you have studied in this chapter to support your explanation.

☐ Academic Vocabulary Review

Here are some academic vocabulary words that were introduced in this chapter. Confirm the words whose meanings you know. Identify the words that are not yet part of your active vocabulary. Relearn the words you need to.

1. abstract	**9.** displayed	**17.** location	**25.** symbol
2. attitudes	**10.** ignore	**18.** maintained	**26.** removed
3. civil	**11.** illustrates	**19.** non-traditional	**27.** revealed
4. contrast	**12.** themes	**20.** occurred	**28.** selected
5. controversial	**13.** injury	**21.** panel	**29.** traditional
6. create	**14.** injuries	**22.** positive	**30.** symbolic
7. cultural	**15.** issue	**23.** reaction	**31.** symbolized
8. design	**16.** job	**24.** site	

WEB POWER

You will find additional exercises related to the content in this chapter at **elt.heinle.com/collegereading**.

Answer key for the puzzle:

		¹T	E	M	P	O	R	A	R	Y	
		²C	R	E	A	T	E	D			
		³S	Y	M	B	O	L	I	C		
	⁴C	I	V	I	L						
		⁵I	G	N	O	R	E				
		⁶D	I	S	P	L	A	Y	E	D	
		⁷P	O	S	I	T	I	V	E		
			⁸L	O	C	A	T	I	O	N	S
			⁹R	E	A	C	T	I	O	N	
¹⁰I	M	A	G	E	S						
¹¹T	H	E	M	E	S						
				¹²C	O	N	T	R	A	S	T

Science and Society: The Ethics of Research

ACADEMIC FOCUS: SCIENCE

Academic Reading Objectives

After completing this chapter, you should be able to:

✓ Check here as you master each objective.

1. Develop critical-thinking skills ☐
2. Improve reading comprehension and gain content knowledge ☐
3. Use new vocabulary orally and in writing ☐
4. Enhance dictionary skills ☐
5. Develop additional study skills ☐

Science Objectives

1. Comprehend vocabulary related to science ☐
2. State the difference between inductive and deductive reasoning ☐
3. Discuss different types of research ☐
4. Explain ethical and unethical issues in scientific research ☐
5. Discuss differences between science and technology ☐

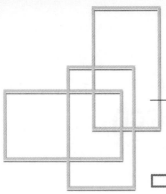

Reading Assignment 1

▭ Getting Ready to Read

EXERCISE 1   **Participating in class discussion**

Discuss the following with your classmates:

1. What do you think is the difference between science and technology?
2. How are they similar?
3. What do scientists do?

▭ Reading the Selection

STRATEGY

Bold Headings

Before you read Selection 1, study the **bold** headings. The headings will help you understand the reading selection. They will help you organize your ideas as you read.

Reading Selection 1

SCIENCE AND TECHNOLOGY

1   Are science and technology identical? Many people think technology is another name for "applied science." It is certainly true that sometimes science and technology overlap. However, the two fields are not identical. There are important differences between science and technology. These differences fall into three categories: 1) goals, 2) methods, and 3) outcomes. Goals are the results that scientists or technicians hope to achieve. Methods are what each group does to achieve the goals. Outcomes are the results that each group achieves.

Goals

2   The people who work in the field of technology are called technicians[1] or engineers.[2] The goal of their work is to create objects, machines, or systems to help humans. Technicians or engineers make objects like tools, or machines like computers, or systems like computer software.[3] These are all things that make our lives better or easier.

3   On the other hand, the main goal of scientists is to look for knowledge. Unlike engineers, scientists are not as concerned about solving the everyday problems we face. They are more interested in advancing human knowledge. Scientists want to know how things work. They want to understand the natural world. A scientist might ask the question, "How old is the universe?" Or they might want to know, "Why do people change their behavior?" Or they may ask, "What causes chemicals to interact?"

Methods

4   The main methods of engineers and technicians are design, invention,[4] and production. These methods match with their goals. Engineers try to gather enough data to make objects, machines, or systems that can solve a problem. They build models of these objects, machines, or systems and test them. They try to find the model that works the best. For example, engineers might want to make a better airplane. They would build a small model[5] of the airplane. Then they would test the small airplane to see how efficient it is.

1. **tech•ni•cian** (tĕk-nĭsh´ən) *n.* A person skilled in a technical field.
2. **en•gi•neer** (ĕn´je-nîr´) *n.* A person trained in a branch of engineering.
3. **com•put•er soft•ware** (kəm-pyoo´tər sôft´wâr´) *n.* Programs, routines, and symbolic languages that control operation of a computer.
4. **in•ven•tion** (ĭn-vĕn´shən) *n.* Something that is produced or created by using the imagination.
5. **mod•el** (mŏd´l) *n.* Small-scale copy representing something.

5   Scientists are more interested in discovery. They search for truth using the scientific method. They do experiments. They develop <u>theories</u> about basic principles. For example, a scientist might ask, "What causes things to fly?" After they ask this question, they make a guess about how flight works. Then they decide what experiments they must use to discovery how flight works.

Outcomes

6   What results do engineers achieve? They solve problems that all human beings face in daily life. They create systems for solving these problems. For example, engineers figure out what to do with waste that goes into water. They build machines to make a city's water safe to drink. Engineers and technicians might also try to help factories. They can help factory workers make more products with less work.

7   What about scientists? What results from their efforts? They try to come up with better <u>definitions</u> and better theories to explain nature. They learn about the age of the universe. They study the smallest particles of life. They make hypotheses about the cause of life on earth. They ask questions about how and why humans behave the way they do.

8   There is a relationship between science and technology. Often, what the scientist discovers in an experiment, the engineer can use in a new invention. In this way, science and technology can work together. But they are not the same thing.

☐ Assessing Your Learning: Science and Technology

Demonstrating Comprehension

One way to help you remember information is to organize it. Study Reading Selection 1 again. Notice that each section has information about technology and science.

EXERCISE 2 Organizing information

Use the information from Reading Selection 1 to complete the chart. Write the goals, methods, and outcomes that go with technology and science. Also write examples for each category. The first one has been done as an example.

	Technology	Science
Goals	Create objects, machines, or systems to help humans.	Look for knowledge
Examples	Tools, machines, computers, computer software	
Methods		
Examples		
Outcomes		
Example		

EXERCISE **3** **Checking comprehension**

Choose the correct answers. Base your choices on Reading Selection 1.

1. Science and technology
   a. are identical.
   b. have some similarities and some differences.
   c. are totally different.

2. Outcomes are
   a. the results that scientists hope to achieve.
   b. what each group does to achieve the goal.
   c. the results that each group achieves.

3. The goal of a scientist is
   a. to experiment with chemicals.
   b. to make our lives easier or better.
   c. to look for knowledge.

4. Which method would an engineer use?
   a. Develop a theory.
   b. Design a new telephone.
   c. Ask questions about nature.

5. Who is most likely to discover a new star?
   a. Scientist
   b. Engineer
   c. Technician

6. Who is most likely to improve a telescope?
   a. Scientist
   b. Technician
   c. Biologist

7. Engineers do all these *except*
   a. figure out what to do with waste that goes into our water.
   b. learn about the age of the universe.
   c. try to help workers produce more and work less.

☐ Learning Vocabulary

EXERCISE 4   Studying academic vocabulary

These words from Reading Selection 1 are commonly found in academic texts. Study the list of words below, and then learn them by following these guidelines:

1. Number a paper from 1 to 16. Copy these words, leaving spaces for definitions. The paragraph location is provided in parentheses next to the word.
2. Write a definition, synonym, or translation for each word you already know.
3. Compare your list with a partner's. Help each other learn new words.
4. Share your list with your classmates. Your instructor can help you define the words you do not know.

1. technology (¶ 1)	**7.** outcomes (¶ 1)	**12.** interact (¶ 3)
2. identical (¶ 1)	**8.** achieve (¶ 1)	**13.** design (¶ 4)
3. overlap (¶ 1)	**9.** create (¶ 2)	**14.** data (¶ 4)
4. categories (¶ 1)	**10.** computers (¶ 2)	**15.** theories (¶ 5)
5. goals (¶ 1)	**11.** chemicals (¶ 3)	**16.** definitions (¶ 7)
6. methods (¶ 1)		

Match each vocabulary word with words that can come before it in a sentence.

1. science and _____	**a.** categories
2. fall into three _____	**b.** computers
3. achieve _____	**c.** interact
4. work to _____	**d.** data
5. machines like _____	**e.** definitions
6. to _____	**f.** theories
7. gather enough _____	**g.** technology
8. develop _____	**h.** goals
9. come up with better _____	**i.** create

EXERCISE 5 Using academic vocabulary

Using the clues below, complete the word puzzle with academic words.

							T			
	¹						T			
		²				E				
		³			C					
		⁴		H						
		⁵		N						
⁶				I						
			⁷	C						
	⁸			I						
		⁹	A							
		¹⁰	N							
	¹¹	S								

Clues

1. The meaning of a word is its _____.

2. To act together

3. Results

4. The ways things are done

5. Exactly the same

6. Groups that things belong to

7. To reach a goal

8. Elements or compounds

9. Information gathered from experiments

10. To act with each other

11. To create a plan or pattern

⬛ Focusing on Science

EXERCISE **6**   Inventing

Engineers and technicians create objects, machines, or systems to help humans. Work with a small group. Discuss the following items with your group.

1. What creative new object, machine, or system can you imagine that might help humans today (for example, a car powered by garbage, a machine that automatically translates different languages)?
2. What would your invention look like? Make a drawing of the invention to show how it works.
3. Describe your invention to the other students.

⬛ Questions for Review

Reading Selection 1 looks at the goals, methods, and outcomes of scientists and technologists. Think about how you could apply these categories to other kinds of work. For example, what goals would an artist have? What methods would an artist use? What outcomes would an artist have?

	Goals	Methods	Outcome
Scientists	Look for knowledge	Do experiments and develop theories	Explain nature
Technologists	Create helpful things	Design invention & production	Create systems & solve problems

EXERCISE 7 **Reflecting on new learning**

Complete the chart. Compare your answers with those of your classmates.
What other kinds of work could you add to this list?

	Goals	Methods	Outcomes
Artist			
Writer			
Historian			
Musician			
Teacher			
Businessperson			

Linking Concepts

EXERCISE 8 **Writing in your reading journal**

Answer the following questions in your reading journal:

1. Would you rather be a scientist, or an engineer or technician?
   Explain your answer.
2. Science and technology have some differences and similarities.
   Explain some of the ways science and technology are the same.

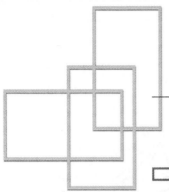

Reading Assignment 2

SCIENTIFIC RESEARCH

⬜ Getting Ready to Read

EXERCISE 9 **Discussing and previewing vocabulary**

Discuss the following items with your classmates:

1. What is scientific research?
2. What do scientists do when they research?
3. What kinds of things do scientists research?
4. Biologists and chemists are scientists. List some other kinds of scientists.
5. What are some things scientists have discovered by research?

Reading Selection 2 talks about how scientists do research. When they do research, scientists use two types of thinking. They use inductive reasoning and deductive reasoning.

A. Inductive reasoning begins when scientists make observations and do experiments. From these observations and experiments, the scientists look for patterns that are similar in each experiment. From these patterns, the scientists make a theory. The pictures below show how scientists think inductively.

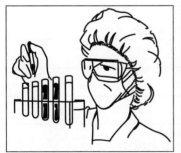

I've got a theory on how that works.

B. Deductive reasoning begins with a theory. Scientists try to prove that the theory is true by making observations or doing experiments. The pictures below show how scientists think deductively.

▢ Reading the Selection

EXERCISE **10** **Understanding two types of reasoning**

As you read Selection 2, look for inductive and deductive reasoning. Write some examples on the lines below. Write the paragraph numbers where you find the examples. If you need help understanding these two types of thinking, look back at the pictures .

1. Inductive reasoning examples: ___Piaget's work . . .___

_____

_____

_____

2. Deductive reasoning examples: _____

_____

_____

_____

Reading Selection 2

SCIENTIFIC RESEARCH

Jean Piaget

1   Scientists can be biologists, chemists, physicists, and psychologists. They study many different things. No matter what they study, scientists use the same steps when they do research. This reading selection explains how scientists do research.

2   Jean Piaget was a famous psychologist. He studied how children develop. He observed his own children. He made notes of his observations.[1] Then he observed more children. He compared his observations. He worked out a theory of how children grow and develop. He tested his theory and wrote about it. Other psychologists repeated his experiments. They added their own observations. Jean Piaget used the steps scientists follow when they do research. These steps are called the "scientific method."

The Scientific Method

3   Science is one way to get knowledge. It is a way to find out about nature. It uses certain procedures to answer questions. These procedures are called the Scientific Method. In science, any theory must have proof[2] to support it.

4   A theory is a statement about how nature works. For example, there is a theory of evolution. This theory says animals changed and developed over many years. Scientists use observations and experiments.[3] These help them to develop theories. The observations and experiments must be objective. Objective means something based on fact. It means something that can be seen or measured. To make sure their theories are true, scientists do experiments.

1. **ob•ser•va•tion** (ŏb′zər-vā′shən) *n.* Act of watching.
2. **proof** (proŏf) *n.* Evidence of truth.
3. **ex•per•i•ment** (ĭk-spĕr′ə-mənt) *n.* Test to find out about or show something.

5   Scientists use the scientific method. One of the steps in the scientific method is to make a hypothesis. A hypothesis is a statement that makes a guess about what is true or not. Then scientists do experiments or make observations to find out if their hypothesis is true or not. Here are the steps in the scientific method.

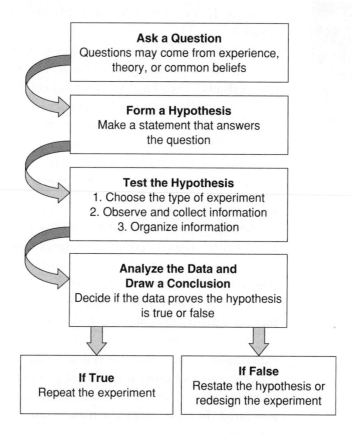

What Are Paradigms?

6   Scientists work within a paradigm. A paradigm is a particular way of looking at the world. For example, some scientists believe that that they must understand how each part of the brain works in order to understand the whole brain. Others believe that they must understand how the parts of the brain connect with each other. A scientist who has the first paradigm will carefully study each part of the brain individually. A scientist who has the second paradigm will focus on connections between the parts.

Where Do Theories Come From?

7   Scientists create theories by studying many examples. They repeat experiments many times. They want to get the same results each time. Scientists look for things these examples have in common. This is called inductive reasoning.[4] Inductive reasoning means studying many examples to create a theory.

8   For example, a biologist takes samples of lake water every day at the same time. He looks at the water under a microscope. He writes down how many microscopic[5] animals are in the water. He also writes down the temperature of the water. Depending on the results,[6] he makes a theory. His theory might be microscopic animals like warm water. The biologist used inductive reasoning. He looked at many examples by taking water samples every day. From those examples, he found a theory. His theory is there are more microscopic animals when the water is warm.

9   Theories cannot usually be proved true. Scientist can't test every possible situation. Even a simple statement such as "crows are black" is not true unless the scientist looks at every crow in the whole world.

How Are Theories Used?

10   Once scientists have a theory, they can test it. For example, the biologist could test his theory that microscopic animals like warm water. He could keep samples of lake water at different temperatures. Then he could measure the number of animals in the water. When scientists test a theory like this it is called deductive reasoning.[7] In deductive reasoning you start from a theory or general statement and see if the examples fit the theory.

Source: Adapted from: *Introduction to Psychology*. McDougal Littell. (2001). pp. 18–21.

4. **in•duc•tive rea•son•ing** (ĭn-dŭk′tĭv rē′zən-ĭng) *n.* Thinking in which a conclusion is reached based on a fact.
5. **mi•cro•scop•ic** (mī′kre-skŏp′ĭk) *n.* Extremely small; too small to be seen with the naked eye.
6. **re•sult** (rĭ-zŭlt′) *n.* Consequence of an action.
7. **de•duc•tive rea•son•ing** (dĭ-dŭk′tĭv rē′zən-ĭng) *n.* Thinking in which a conclusion is reached by reasoning.

▭ Assessing Your Learning: Scientific Research

Demonstrating Comprehension

EXERCISE **11** **Checking comprehension**

Read the following statements. If the statement is true, write T. If the statement is false, write F and change the statement to make it true. The first one has been done for you as an example.

1. __*f*__ Jean Piaget's theory on how children develop came from
observations of children.
~~experiments he did with children.~~

2. _____ Biologists and psychologists use the same basic steps when they do research.

3. _____ Jean Piaget used the scientific method.

4. _____ Scientists do not have to prove their theories.

5. _____ Experiments and observations are used to prove theories are true.

6. _____ Scientists must work within the same paradigm.

7. _____ Deductive reasoning means studying many examples to create a theory.

8. _____ Theories are usually proved true.

9. _____ Inductive reasoning starts with a theory; it tests the theory with experiments.

10. _____ Once scientists have a theory, they no longer need to test it.

11. _____ Theories are general statements.

EXERCISE 12   **Increasing memorization with headings**

Headings can help you remember information from a reading. Write the information you remember from each section under the headings listed below. Do this without looking back at Reading Selection 2.

1. **The Scientific Method**

   _____

   _____

   _____

   _____

2. **What Are Paradigms?**

   _____

   _____

   _____

   _____

3. **Where Do Theories Come From?**

   _____

   _____

   _____

   _____

4. **How Are Theories Used?**

   _____

   _____

   _____

   _____

Now compare what you remember with what a partner remembers. Add to your list any details you forgot.

🔲 Learning Vocabulary

EXERCISE 13   **Studying academic vocabulary**

These words from Reading Selection 2 are commonly found in academic texts. Study the list of words below, and then learn them by following these guidelines.

1. Number a paper from 1 to 11. Copy these words, leaving spaces for definitions. The paragraph location is provided in parentheses next to each word.
2. Write a definition, synonym, or translation for each word you already know.
3. Compare your list with a partner's. Help each other learn new words.
4. Share your list with your classmates. Your instructor can help you define the words you do not know.

1. psychologists (¶ 1)	**5.** procedures (¶ 3)	**9.** individually (¶ 6)
2. research (¶ 1)	**6.** objective (¶ 4)	**10.** focus (¶ 6)
3. theory (¶ 2)	**7.** hypothesis (¶ 5)	**11.** create (¶ 7)
4. method (¶ 2)	**8.** paradigm (¶ 6)	

EXERCISE 14   **Using academic vocabulary**

Complete the following sentences with the correct academic vocabulary word from the list in Exercise 13.

1. A _____ is a way of looking at things.

2. The scientific method requires scientist to follow the correct

   _____.

3. _____ is a study of information about something.

4. A scientific guess about what is true or not is a _____.

5. If something is _____, it is based on facts.

6. To make or invent something is to _____.

7. A _____ studies human behavior.

8. A scientist must _____ on a problem.

9. A _____ can never be proved true.

10. You must do the test _____ by yourself.

11. A _____ is a way of doing something.

EXERCISE 15   **Working with word families**

Some words have similar base words but are used in different forms. Find these words in Reading Selection 2. The paragraph in which each is found is written in parentheses. Write your own definitions for the words. Base your definitions on how the words are used in the reading.

observe

1. observations (¶ 2) _____

_____

2. observed (¶ 2) _____

_____

prove

3. proof (¶ 3) _____

_____

4. proved (¶ 9) _____

_____

connect

5. connect (¶ 6) _____

_____

6. connections (¶ 6) _____

_____

scope

7. microscope (¶ 8) _____

_____

8. microscopic (¶ 8) _____

_____

EXERCISE 16 **Determining definitions from context**

Sometimes the definition of a new word can be found right in the reading text. This makes it easy to learn new words. Define the words below by noticing the context. The paragraph location is included next to each item. Scan Reading Selection 2 to find each one. The first one is done for you as an example.

> Science is one way to get knowledge. It is a way to find out about nature. It uses certain procedures to answer questions. These procedures are called the **Scientific Method**. In science, any theory must have proof to support it.

1. Scientific Method (¶ 3) _the procedures used by scientists. It is a way of proving a theory._

2. theory of evolution (¶ 4) _a theory about. . ._

3. objective (¶ 4) _____

4. hypothesis (¶ 5) _____

5. paradigm (¶ 6) _____

6. inductive reasoning (¶ 7) _____

7. deductive reasoning (¶ 10) _____

▭ **Focusing on Science**

EXERCISE 17   **Applying inductive and deductive reasoning**

Work in a group of three or four students. Turn back to Reading Selection 2, "Research on Intelligence," in Chapter 1. Paragraph 1 of that reading lists five theories about intelligence. With your group, complete the following tasks:

1. Write the five theories. Leave space below each theory.

   a. _____

   _____

   b. _____

   _____

   c. _____

   _____

   d. _____

   _____

   e. _____

   _____

2. Make a list of observations or experiments you think scientists could do to test each of those theories.

   a. _____

   _____

   b. _____

   _____

   c. _____

   _____

   d. _____

   _____

   e. _____

   _____

3. Would the scientists be using inductive or deductive reasoning with each of the five theories? Explain your answer.

1. _____

2. _____

3. _____

4. _____

5. _____

▭ Questions for Review

EXERCISE 18 **Reflecting on new learning**

Work with a group of three or four other students. Discuss the following questions:

1. What are the steps of the scientific method?
2. Why is it important for scientists to follow those steps?
3. What would happen if they didn't follow the steps?
4. What scientific questions would you like to know the answers to?

Write your question, using the first three steps in the scientific method:

a. Ask a question.
b. Form a hypothesis.
c. Test the hypothesis. (For this step, explain what observations or experiments you could use to test the hypothesis.)

▭ Linking Concepts

EXERCISE 19 **Writing in your reading journal**

Answer the following questions in your reading journal:

1. Write your personal response to question 2, 3, or 4 from Exercise 18.
2. In your journal, create a chart, picture, or diagram that shows the difference between inductive and deductive reasoning.

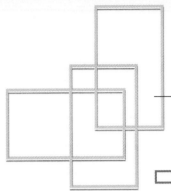

Reading Assignment 3

ETHICAL ISSUES IN SCIENTIFIC RESEARCH

Getting Ready to Read

Sometimes it is difficult to understand a word's definition. For instance, the definition for the word *ethics* is difficult to understand because some words in the definition are difficult. The definition entry for *ethics* includes the words *moral, conduct,* and *principles.* If you are unclear about the meanings of those words, you might also have to look up their definitions before you can understand the word *ethics.* This task makes understanding the original definition more difficult.

EXERCISE 20 Previewing vocabulary

Study the words below and their definitions. Then break down the definition by defining or explaining the words it includes. The first one is done for you as an example. Later, as you read, look for these new vocabulary words you have learned.

1. **Ethics.** (ĕth´ĭk)(*n.*) A system of moral or correct conduct, moral principles. *She has good business ethics.*

   Moral. (adjective) Relating to what is right or wrong

   Conduct. (noun) Behavior, one's manners.

   Principles. (plural noun) A rule, policy belief.

2. **Bias.** (bī´əs) (*n.*) General tendency. *He has a bias against eating vegetables.*

   _____

   _____

   _____

3. **Risk.** (rĭsk) (*v.*) To put something important in danger. *Firefighters risk their lives every day.*

_____

_____

_____

4. **Benefit.** (bĕn´ə-fĭt) (*n.*) A positive result. *Good health is a benefit of daily exercise.*

_____

_____

_____

▭ Reading the Selection

Reading Selection 3

ETHICAL ISSUES IN SCIENTIFIC RESEARCH

Bias in Research

1   At a party, you notice a mother of five, a doctor, a blond in an evening dress, and a millionaire. Which of those people would you most want to talk to? Which would you least want to talk to? What if all four are the same person?

2   Most of us have certain beliefs about people. These beliefs are based on such things as the way people dress, the groups they belong to, or whether they are male or female. The ideas we have about something can cause us to be biased. For example, some people think females are better than males. They might look at their actions differently from someone who has the opposite opinion. Depending on the biases they have, scientists might interpret the same behavior in different ways. Bias is anything that distorts or misrepresents the data or facts in an experiment. Scientists must not be biased.

3   Bias is one of the ethical issues in research. If someone is ethical, it means he or she has moral[1] or correct behavior.

Other Ethical Issues in Research

4   Besides bias, scientists face other ethical issues. Some experiments can be considered unethical. One example of unethical research is an experiment about prejudice. Some teachers have done this experiment. For one day, all of the students who wear a certain color of clothes are treated badly. The teachers tell the other students to ignore them or to act prejudiced[2] against them. Many students agree that this experiment helps them understand how bad prejudice can be. However, there are possible problems with this experiment:

- Students who are not normally prejudiced become upset when they have to act that way.
- Students who are treated badly feel bad for a long time even though the experiment was "pretend."

Risks[3] and Benefits

5   Scientists must be careful with experiments that use human subjects. Some experiments encourage people to behave in ways that are not comfortable for them. Or the experiment may affect their health or emotions. Some scientists say that these experiments are necessary to learn about humans. Others say that the risks are too great. Who is correct?

1. **mo·ral** (môr´əl) *adj.* Relating to the judgment of the goodness and badness of human action.
2. **prej·u·diced** (prĕj´e-dĭs) *adj.* Having an unfair judgment of something or someone before one knows the facts.
3. **risk** (rĭsk) *n.* Possibility of suffering harm or loss.

6   These scientists disagree because they have different values. Some scientists value increasing knowledge. Others value protecting individuals. Sometimes the knowledge might lead to a theory that would save or improve many lives. It might be worth the risk. For example, a new drug might cure cancer.[4] However, the drug could also be harmful. Should a doctor encourage the cancer patient to take the drug? The doctor must decide what is more important-possible harm or finding a cure for cancer. The doctor must decide if the risk is worth the benefit. It is important to compare the risks and benefits of any experiment that uses humans or animals.

Should Animals Be Used in Research?

7   Many scientists use animals in research. Scientists argue that the benefits gained from animal research are more important than the rights of the animals. They point out that many human diseases have been eliminated because of animal research. Without this research many humans could have died.

8   Others argue that animals have rights. They believe scientists cannot trade animal rights for the benefit of people. These people believe that it is important to protect animals. They point out that animals cannot tell people if they are being hurt.

9   Animals have been used in medical experiments. This causes animals pain and even death. Animals have also been used to test products like soaps and cosmetics.[5] This can also cause animals problems like pain, blindness and death. In laboratories animals are not always treated well. They may not have enough food or a comfortable place to live.

10   Today there are ethical rules that scientists must use when working with animals. The scientists must prove that animal experiments are the best way to test their hypotheses. They must try to prevent pain for animals. They must take care of the animals. They must give them proper food and a comfortable place to live.

11   What do you think? Should animals be used in research?

Source: Adapted from *Introduction to Psychology.* McDougal Littell. (2001), pp. 20, 30–33

4. **can•cer** (kăn′sər) *n.* Any of various diseases in which body cells grow in an abnormal way.
5. **cos•met•ic** (kŏz-mĕt′ĭk) *n.* Preparation designed to beautify the body.

☐ Assessing Your Learning: Ethical Issues in Scientific Research

Demonstrating Comprehension

EXERCISE 21 Checking comprehension

Answer the questions based on the reading selection.

1. What are some things that can cause people to be biased?
2. Explain how the person described in paragraph 1 could be the same person.
3. How can bias affect scientists?
4. Why is it important for scientists to be unbiased?
5. Do you think the experiment described in paragraph 4 is ethical or unethical? Explain your answer.
6. What are some risks of human research?
7. What are some benefits of human research?
8. Why must scientists follow ethical rules when working with animals?
9. What ethical rules must scientists follow when working with animals?

☐ Questions for Review

EXERCISE 22 Discussing in small groups

Discuss the following questions in groups of three or four:

1. If animals are not used in research, how should a new medication be tested before it is given to humans?
2. In what other occupations must people remain unbiased?
3. Why should someone risk her or his life while participating in an experiment to test a new medication?

☐ Learning Vocabulary

EXERCISE 23 Studying academic vocabulary

These words from Reading Selection 3 are commonly found in academic texts. Study the list of words below, and then learn them by following these guidelines:

1. Number a paper from 1 to 14. Copy these words, leaving spaces for definitions. The paragraph location is provided in parentheses next to each word.
2. Write a definition, synonym, or translation for each word you already know.
3. Compare your list with a partner's. Help each other learn new words.
4. Share your list with your classmates. Your instructor can help you define the words you do not know.

1. ethical (title)	**8.** ignore (¶ 4)
2. issues (title)	**9.** normally (¶ 4)
3. bias (heading)	**10.** benefits (heading)
4. research (heading)	**11.** affect (¶ 5)
5. interpret (¶ 2)	**12.** individuals (¶ 6)
6. distort (¶ 2)	**13.** theory (¶ 6)
7. data (¶ 2)	**14.** medical (¶ 9)

Match each vocabulary word with the words that can follow it in a sentence.

1. ethical (title) _____	**a.** research
2. bias (heading) _____	**b.** the facts
3. scientific _____	**c.** individuals
4. interpret (¶ 2) _____	**d.** issues
5. distorts (¶ 2) _____	**e.** against
6. affect (¶ 5) _____	**f.** experiments
7. protect _____	**g.** data
8. medical _____	**h.** their emotions

POWER GRAMMAR

Noticing Collocations

Many times, words in English are grouped together in phrases. You can improve your vocabulary by remembering not only words but also other words that are commonly found after those words.

EXERCISE 24   **Practicing collocation**

The numbered list shows some verbs from Reading Selection 3 and the prepositions that usually follow them. Notice that not all prepositions go with all verbs. For example, in English we say "based on" or "based in," but we don't say "based to" or "based against."

   a. Study the groups of words.
   b. Find the **bold** words in Reading Selection 3 and circle them. The paragraph in which each is found is written in parentheses.
   c. The list also has some other common prepositions that go with these words. Say the words out loud together. For example say "based on," "based in." Try to remember the words as a group.
   d. Notice how the preposition changes the meaning of the word.
   e. Practice using the words and prepositions by writing a sentence with each. If you are unsure of the meaning, ask your instructor.

   1. based **on** (¶ 2); based in
   2. belong **to** (¶ 2)
   3. depending **on** (¶ 2)
   4. prejudiced **against** (¶ 4); prejudiced toward
   5. learn **about** (¶ 5); learn through
   6. lead **to** (¶ 6); lead into
   7. gained **from** (¶ 7)
   8. for the benefit **of** (¶ 8); of benefit to
   9. take care **of** (¶ 10)

☐ Focusing on Science

EXERCISE 25   **Evaluating ethics**

The two reading passages that follow describe real research studies that scientists have done. Read each passage. Then decide if you think the research study was ethical or not. Explain why you think it is ethical or unethical.

1. WOULD YOU CONFORM?

1 Conformity means changing attitudes or behaviors that reflect the group you are a member of. Groups have a very strong effect on us. They pressure us to conform. Why do we need to go along with the group? There are two main reasons. We want to be liked. We want to be right.

2 Psychologist Solomon Asch did a series of experiments to explore what happens when the pressure to conform conflicts with a person's perception of reality.

3 In his experiments, Asch staged a fake (false) experiment. The subjects in the experiment were told to compare three different lines drawn on a card. The subjects were supposed to choose two lines that were the same length. A group of seven students were shown the line at the same time.

4 Six of the students were actually Asch's students. The true objective of the experiment was to see whether the seventh student would believe his or her own eyes. The experimenters wanted to see if the student would insist on the correct answer even if the other six students gave a different, incorrect answer.

5 Asch found that 75 percent of the students he tested went along with the other six students at least some of the time. However, when students wrote their answers in private instead of saying them out loud, they were less likely to conform or go along with the other six students.

6 Asch's experiment has important implications because it shows how powerful the desire to conform is. The desire to conform is so strong that we may find ourselves supporting ideas or behaviors that we don't really agree with. We might even support ideas that are morally wrong.

   a. Do you think Asch's experiment is ethical?
   b. Is it ethical to lie to the student about the purpose of the experiment?
   c. Explain why you think this experiment is ethical or unethical.

Source: Adapted from Nexttext. (2001). *Introduction to Psychology.* Elgin, IL: McDougal Littell, p. 314.

2. PRISONERS AND GUARDS

1   Psychologists Craig Haney, Curtis Banks, and Philip Zimbardo wanted to find out how the prison system affects how people act with each other. They used male college students with no history of emotional problems. They randomly assigned half of the student to play the role of guards and half to play prisoners in a fake prison.

2   The experiment was to last for two weeks. "Guards" wore uniforms. They enforced prison rules, gave prisoners meals, and let them have a few recreational opportunities. They worked eight hours at a time. After their eight hours of work was finished, they could go home. "Prisoners" wore prison clothes. They were identified by numbers rather than by their names. They had to stay in prison night and day.

3   In just two days, the roles began to control the students. Before the week was out, half of the "prisoners" had to be released early because they had extreme anxiety and depression. The "guards" had taken away the "prisoners'" privileges. They bothered, humiliated, or punished prisoners. The experiment was stopped after only six days. The experimenters feared for the safety of the students.

4   This experiment shows why certain problems develop in some prisons. However, it also shows how easy it is for social roles to change our behavior.

   a. Do you think the "Prisoners and Guards" experiment is ethical?

   _____

   _____

   b. Do you think the experiment should have been stopped in only six days? Why or why not?

   _____

   _____

   c. Explain why you think this experiment is ethical or unethical.

   _____

   _____

Source: Adapted from Nexttext. (2001). Introduction to Psychology. Elgin, IL: McDougal Littell, p. 322.

▭ Questions for Review

EXERCISE 26 **Reflecting on new learning**

Work in a group of three or four students. Brainstorm with your group. In the chart below, write a list of reasons for and against animal research. Compare your list with those of other groups. Do you think animals should have rights? Explain your opinions to your classmates.

Animal research	
Reasons for	**Reasons against**
1.	1.
2.	2.
3.	3.

▭ Linking Concepts

EXERCISE 27 **Writing in your reading journal**

Answer the following questions in your reading journal:

1. Ethics are not just important in science. They are also important in business. Explain why business ethics are important.

2. Do you think animals have rights? Defend your answer.

3. Do you think human research is necessary? Explain why you would or would not participate in a human research project.

▭ Assessing Your Learning at the End of a Chapter

Revisiting Objectives

Return to the first page of this chapter to revisit the chapter objectives. Put a check mark next to the objectives you feel confident about. Review the material in the chapter you need to learn better. When you are ready, take the practice test in Exercise 28. These items reflect the chapter objectives and come from all three reading selections.

▭ Practicing for a Chapter Test

EXERCISE 28   **Reviewing comprehension**

Check your comprehension of important material in this chapter by answering the following questions. First, write notes to answer the questions without looking back at the readings. Then, use the readings and exercises to check your answers and revise them. Write your final answers in complete sentences on separate paper.

1. What is the relationship between science and technology?

2. Describe goals, methods, and outcomes.

3. The example given about Jean Piaget is based on which type of scientific thinking? How do you know?

4. What is a paradigm?

5. Describe some ethical issues scientists must deal with.

6. How can bias influence the results of an experiment?

7. What was the purpose of Asch's experiment?

8. How can someone's role affect her or his behavior?

▭ Academic Vocabulary Review

Here are some academic vocabulary words that were introduced in this chapter. Confirm the words whose meanings you know. Identify the words that are not yet part of your active vocabulary. Relearn the words you need to.

1. achieve	**10.** definitions	**19.** individuals	**28.** outcomes
2. affect	**11.** design	**20.** individually	**29.** overlap
3. benefits	**12.** distorts	**21.** interact	**30.** paradigm
4. bias	**13.** ethical	**22.** interpret	**31.** paradigms
5. categories	**14.** focus	**23.** issues	**32.** procedure
6. chemicals	**15.** goals	**24.** medical	**33.** research
7. computers	**16.** hypothesis	**25.** methods	**34.** echnology
8. create	**17.** identical	**26.** normally	**35.** theories
9. data	**18.** ignore	**27.** objective	**36.** theory

WEB POWER

You can find additional exercises related to the content in this chapter at **elt.heinle.com/collegereading.**